pp.

13-18
68-71
108-123
153

PELICAN BOOKS

Thomas Jefferson On Democracy

*Selected and Arranged
With an Introduction by*

SAUL K. PADOVER

PUBLISHED BY
PENGUIN BOOKS, INC.
NEW YORK

COPYRIGHT, 1939, BY D. APPLETON-CENTURY COMPANY, INC

All rights reserved. This book, or parts thereof, must not be reproduced in any form without permission of the publisher.

Published by Penguin Books, Inc.,
And reprinted by arrangement with
D. Appleton-Century Company, Inc.

FIRST PELICAN BOOKS EDITION, DECEMBER, 1946

Penguin Books, Inc., 245 Fifth Avenue, New York 16, N. Y.
Penguin Books Limited, Harmondsworth, Middlesex, England

PRINTED IN THE UNITED STATES OF AMERICA

About This Book

Although Thomas Jefferson's name is closely linked with the idea as well as the reality of American democracy, Jefferson himself wrote no treatise or essay on the subject, and consciously abstained from a systematic exposition of his thoughts on politics and society. What we know of Jefferson's superbly fertile mind, as Saul K. Padover points out in his Preface, is derived mainly from his letters.

From these letters, and other sources—both published and unpublished—Padover has extracted the essence of Jefferson's views on democracy. He has arranged them topically, under the chapter titles "Natural Rights of Man," "Principles of Democracy," "The Constitution," "Political Economy," "Social Welfare," "Religion," and "Foreign Affairs," and he has woven them into an integrated whole. Except for his illuminating Introduction, Padover has added no text of his own, nor has he altered anything of Jefferson's thought. The book is entirely Jefferson's.

It is a book which for the first time reveals Jefferson in his full stature as a political thinker, and as a commentator on the men and events related to the democratic experiment of which he was in large part the creator. Padover himself says: ". . . the reader who will want to give himself the pleasure of perusing the book or browsing through it will make the delightful discovery of a subtle spirit capable sometimes of the indignation of a Swift, and, more often, of the prose rhythm of a Bacon. More perhaps than any other man of his time, Jefferson embodied the thoughts and hopes of a libertarian age, its belief in human goodness, its faith in progress, its trust in science and the enlightenment of reason. The editor feels that this book is timely and much-needed. Today more than ever we need guidance and hope. The editor hopes that Jefferson's countrymen will want to renew their acquaintance with the author of the Declaration of Independence."

PREFACE

Thomas Jefferson, a cool and poised statesman, measured his public utterances with a view to achieving a maximum of political effect. Butt of a hostile and vicious press, and highly sensitive to the abuse of his person and ideas, Jefferson carefully refrained from giving his enemies any opening for verbal bombardment. "From a very early period in my life," he wrote to James Monroe in 1796, "I had laid it down as a rule of conduct, never to write a word for the public papers."

More than that. This articulate statesman-philosopher consciously abstained from a systematic development of his thoughts on politics and society. Although his name is immortally linked with the idea and the reality of American democracy, Jefferson wrote no treatise or essay on the subject. To Van der Kemp he wrote in 1816: "You ask if I have ever published anything but the *Notes on Virginia?* Nothing but official State papers."

Whence, then, do we obtain our knowledge of Jefferson's ideas on democracy? What we know of Jefferson's superbly fertile mind we derive mainly from his letters. Cautious though he was in his public utterances, in his private correspondence he revealed his glowing hopes, his incredibly many-sided culture, his ample imagination, with little hindrance and small restraint. His letters, written from the fulness of a capacious mind and generous heart, are a permanent heritage of American democracy.

The selections from Jefferson's letters and other writings, arranged in this book so as to make an integrated whole, are, most of them, strikingly quotable. This, the editor wishes to insist, is not an anthology but a unified work, reasoned and carefully constructed. Every word in the text is Jefferson's own, and the reader who will want to give himself the pleasure of perusing the book or browsing through it will make the delightful discovery of a subtle spirit capable sometimes of the indignations of a Swift and, more often, of the prose rhythm of a Bacon. More perhaps than any other man of his time, Jefferson embodied the thoughts and hopes of a libertarian age, its belief in human goodness, its faith in progress, its trust in science and the enlightenment of reason.

The editor feels that this book is timely and much-needed. To-day more than ever we need guidance and hope. The editor hopes that Jefferson's countrymen will want to renew their acquaintance with the author of the Declaration of Independence.   S. K. P.

CONTENTS

PREFACE V
INTRODUCTION 1

Chapter
I. NATURAL RIGHTS OF MAN 13
II. PRINCIPLES OF DEMOCRACY 19
    CREDO 19
      i. ADVANTAGES OF DEMOCRACY 19
      ii. AMERICAN DEMOCRACY 27
      iii. PRINCIPLES 31
      iv. REPUBLICANISM 39
      v. POLITICAL PARTIES 42
III. THE CONSTITUTION 46
      i. DIVISION OF POWERS 46
      ii. BILL OF RIGHTS 47
      iii. STATES' RIGHTS 52
      iv. THE PRESIDENCY 55
      v. JUDICIARY 61
      vi. SUBJECT TO CHANGE 66
IV. POLITICAL ECONOMY 68
      i. AGRICULTURE AND COMMERCE 68
      ii. PUBLIC DEBT 71
      iii. TAXATION 74
      iv. BANKING 76
V. SOCIAL WELFARE 79
      i. CLASSES 79
      ii. EDUCATION 87
      iii. PRESS 92
      iv. MINORITIES: NEGROES 98
      v. MINORITIES: INDIANS 103
      vi. IMMIGRATION 107
VI. RELIGION 108
    CREDO 108
      i. TOLERATION 108
      ii. CRITICISM OF CHRISTIANITY 117
      iii. INDIVIDUAL SECTS 118
      iv. CHARACTER OF JESUS 120
      v. PERSONAL FAITH 122
VII. FOREIGN AFFAIRS 123
      i. WAR 123
      ii. NO ENTANGLEMENT 126
      iii. ENGLAND 133
      iv. FRANCE 138
      v. SOUTH AMERICA 144
APPENDIX I: AXIOMS AND DICTA 149
APPENDIX II: OPINION OF CONTEMPORARIES . . . 172
INDEX 184

INTRODUCTION

THIS BOOK is at least a century and a half overdue. Although Jefferson may be considered the St. Paul of American democracy and although he was a prolific writer endowed with extraordinary verbal facility, he never systematically formulated his thoughts on democracy in any one book or even essay.

Jefferson's ideas are embodied in scattered writings, particularly in his superb letters. It is mainly from these letters and the public papers that this book is constructed. The editor has added nothing of his own, nor altered anything of Jefferson's thought. No attempt has been made to resolve occasional contradictions or to omit ideas—in the field of economics, for example—where the editor ventures to disagree with Jefferson. This book is entirely Jefferson's.

It was in his letters that the author of the Declaration of Independence expressed his thoughts and helped to shape those of his generation. He corresponded with hundreds of people in America and in Europe. Throughout his life he wrote about twenty-five thousand letters, an amazing feat considering that Jefferson was also active in politics and farming. Letter-writing was to Jefferson what public speeches, the press conference, and the radio are to statesmen to-day. Through his letters Jefferson spoke to the nation and by means of letters he stimulated his followers. A poor public speaker, Jefferson avoided the platform and sought the desk. Instead of delivering a speech, no matter how salutary it might have been politically, he would write a letter, which he knew would be read publicly. Such letters he wrote for conscious political effect, as means of educating the nation in democracy, or "sowing useful truths," as he phrased it.

The subject of democracy is one of perpetual interest and permanent importance, especially in the United States. The editor has been impressed by the unfortunate ignorance of the meaning and function of democracy that prevails in many sections of our population. This is notably true among so-called intellectuals. Our schools cannot be too severely condemned for this situation; they—particularly the historians and political scientists—have failed in their primary function, that of educating our citizens in the history and significance of American democracy. The editor has met intellectuals who know everything about Russia, or Germany, or Italy, and nothing about the American Constitution; he has known writers and professional people who are experts on Marxism or Fascism, but to whom Jefferson and Madison are mere names of men who lived in the eighteenth century. Such general ignorance, or misunderstanding, of Jeffersonian thought is particularly unfortunate, for the author of the Declaration of Independence is still the embodiment not only of the American dream of liberty and equality but also of mankind's libertarian ideals.

Many Americans are inclined to forget that the priceless heritage of democracy which they enjoy to-day had to be won in hard battle, and that it took generations of effort to establish viable democratic institutions on this continent. Democracy is not a spontaneous gift of the gods. If we are not wise and enlightened, we may not be a democracy in the future. To be preserved, every value must be fought for. In the past the struggle for freedom was won by those who had the brain and the will to be free. Foremost among these master-builders of democracy was, of course, Thomas Jefferson, an unexampled combination of scientist, writer, scholar, administrator, and at the same time the most successful political figure of his day. Despite his shyness he was a fighting man of superb caliber, a man of steel clothed in homespun. In retrospect he appears more and more as a seer in the Biblical sense, a prophet who fulfilled a dream.

What, then, is the meaning of democracy? To Jefferson the core of democracy was the idea of liberty. It should be remembered that he was a product of his age, a student of eighteenth-century philosophy and an observer of the eighteenth-century political scene. But while his reading came from Europe, his feet were on the free soil of America. He was struck, therefore, by the discrepancy between the European philosophers' concept of humanity's natural right to liberty and the actual state of human degradation that surrounded them. A son of a self-taught and independent Virginia farmer, Jefferson could not understand that curiously masochistic mysticism which had made Europeans the frequently willing slaves of their masters. A rationalist and a lover of nature, he was determined that the twin enemies of mankind, obscurantism and tyranny, should never be permitted to take root in the soil of America. In the year when Jefferson was elected third President of the United States, he wrote to his friend Dr. Rush, "I have sworn upon the altar of God eternal hostility against every form of tyranny over the mind of man."

European conditions, which through English rule also affected America, gave Jefferson's thought its uncompromising libertarian bent. Nine-tenths of European mankind was poor and enslaved so that one-tenth could live in liberty and luxury. Even as late as 1826, a few days before he died, Jefferson wrote, with a bitterness that was unusual for him, "The mass of mankind has not been born with saddles on their backs, nor a favored few booted and spurred, ready to ride them legitimately, by the grace of God." Looking over the European scene, what did Jefferson see? England, where a corrupt nobility ruled through an unbalanced monarch. Prussia, dominated by a competent despot to be succeeded by an incompetent one ("a hog in body as well as in mind"). Russia, an enormous prison-house for serfs under the lash of semi-Oriental tyrants. Austria, half-feudal, struggling vainly to throw off aristocracy and clericalism. France, in an agony of misgovernment and poverty, sliding into the abyss of revolution and anarchy. Wherever Jefferson looked in Europe he saw nothing but examples of tyranny and despair.

"While in Europe," he relates, "I often amused myself with contemplating the characters of the then reigning sovereigns.... Louis XVI was a fool.... The King of Spain was a fool, and of Naples the same. They passed their lives in hunting.... The King of Sardinia was a fool.... The Queen of Portugal ... was an idiot by nature. And so was the King of Denmark.... The King of Prussia, successor to the great Frederick, was a mere hog in body as well as in mind. Gustavus of Sweden and Joseph of Austria, were really crazy, and George of England ... was in straight waistcoat.... These animals had become without mind and powerless."

This negative influence of Europe upon Jefferson's thinking and upon American democracy cannot be too strongly emphasized. Europe was socially cruel and politically unjust, and Europe's children crossed thousands of miles of ocean in order to escape from intolerable conditions. "Europe," Jefferson once said, "is a first idea, a crude production, before the maker knew his trade, or had made up his mind as to what he wanted." By implication, America must be an improvement upon the first rough model.

Jefferson's residence in France as American ambassador further deepened his aversion for caste and absolutism. The poverty and suffering in that country filled him with indignation. "Of twenty millions of people supposed to be in France," he wrote from Paris, "I am of opinion there are nineteen millions more wretched, more accursed in every circumstance of human existence than the most conspicuously wretched individual of the whole United States." He knew that the reason for this unnecessary wretchedness was a "bad form of government."

America must never tread the anguished path of Europe, where, Jefferson wrote, the governments are those of "kites over pigeons." Only those who saw Europe could fully appreciate the paradise that America really was. A trip to Europe, so Jefferson wrote to James Monroe in 1785, "will make you adore your own country, its soil, its climate, its equality, liberty, laws, people, and manners." "My God!" he exclaimed, "how little do my countrymen know what precious blessings they are in possession of, and which no other people on earth enjoy."

Here, on the western hemisphere, was a new land and a citizenry not yet demoralized by hereditary inequality. With a population uncorrupted and unchained, and living for the most part on rich and uninfeudated soil, it was possible to build a new society that would not repeat the tragic experience of Europe. Jefferson, moreover, was brought up in what was then frontier territory, and his neighbors, the men he knew and respected, were self-reliant individualists who had carved out their own freeholds without benefit of lord or abbot.

The basic social fact in Jefferson's day, as it is in our day, was the problem of government. Almost every social ill derived ultimately from the nature and function of the State. There were few limits to the cruelties and degradations that a bad government could inflict upon its subjects, who, in Jefferson's day, were largely without political rights, and therefore helpless. To Jefferson it was axiomatic that where the citizens have no right to control the government the result is a society of wolves ruling over sheep. Jefferson could not see that there was even room for argument on this point. Even the worst popular government was preferable to the most glorious autocratic one, for men, Jefferson held, have the natural privilege of committing errors, and, if let alone, their common sense would soon rectify mistakes. Jefferson regarded it as a self-evident proposition that the best government was the one in which the citizens have the most freedom, even to the point of reducing that government to semi-impotency. By the same token, a powerful government was inevitably bad, because sooner rather than later it ceases to be a servant and becomes a master of the citizens who created it.

Jefferson had no illusions about the nature of government.

As a realistic reader of history—like Voltaire, he read history for the lessons it taught rather than for entertainment—Jefferson looked at government in general with cool, skeptical eyes. So, incidentally, did many of his American contemporaries, especially those who were active in the making of the Constitution. Jefferson feared government as a potential menace but accepted it as a necessary evil. Society, he realized, required some sort of regulation, and the individual needed a certain amount of freedom; and since these two requirements appeared mutually exclusive, the conflict between order and liberty seemed irreconcilable. Historically, Jefferson well knew, governments always encroached upon the individual's freedom, sometimes by means of coercive laws and sometimes by means of naked violence. That few rulers ever exercised power for the genuine benefit of the ruled was a proposition almost self-evident. In one of his most revealing sentences Jefferson once admitted that if he had to choose between despotism and anarchism he would prefer anarchism. "Were it made a question, whether no law, as among the savage Americans (Indians), or too much law, as among the civilized Europeans, submits man to the greatest evil, one who has seen both conditions of existence would pronounce it to the last." And he added a phrase that is even more applicable to Europe to-day than it was in his time—"The sheep are happier of themselves, than under the care of the wolves."

Since the inexorable tendency of governments was to deteriorate into tyrannies, the problem before men of Jefferson's generation was how to keep a necessary social servant from growing into a monster. How, in other words, could one prevent government from encroaching upon liberty?

"There are rights," Jefferson wrote in 1789, "which it is useless to surrender to the government, and which governments have yet always been found to invade. These are the rights of thinking, and publishing our thoughts by speaking or writing; the right of free commerce; the right of personal freedom."

To Jefferson government was entirely subservient to life and liberty, and without the latter there could be no pursuit of happiness. A powerful state that would control men's thoughts and action, Jefferson wrote to James Monroe in 1782, would "annihilate the blessing of existence" and would make men feel "that it were better they had never been born."

The solution lay in self-government. Men must be guaranteed their right to elect and to control their public officials, not as a matter of expediency or favor but as a function endowed by nature. Men, Jefferson argued (this was good eighteenth-century doctrine held by many other distinguished minds), were born with a number of *inalienable* rights, "among these are life, liberty and the pursuit of happiness." Among these *natural* rights there is also the right of self-government.

"Every man, and every body of men on earth," Jefferson explained to President Washington in 1790, "possess the right of self-government. They receive it with their being from the hand of nature. Individuals exercise it by their single will; collections of men by that of their majority; for the law of the majority is the natural law of every society of men."

Critics of democracy argued that men were not capable of governing themselves. Jefferson dismissed the argument against democracy in two brief sentences. "Sometimes it is said that man cannot be trusted with the government of himself. Can he, then, be trusted with the government of others?" Nor would Jefferson accept a half-hearted, partial democracy under the tutelage of some person or group. "No, my friend," he wrote to Joseph Cabell, "the way to have good and safe government, is not to trust it all to one, but to divide it among the many." And to his French friend Dupont de Nemours: "We both consider the people as our children.... But you love them as infants whom you are afraid to trust without nurses, and I as adults whom I freely leave to self-government." Professor Charles E. Merriam has called this one of the best statements of democratic principles.

Jefferson had confidence in human character and trusted the "common sense of mankind." Men who rule themselves may commit mistakes, but they have a chance to correct them. But men who are ruled have no way out except suffering in patience or violence. "I have such reliance on the good sense of the body of the people and the honesty of their leaders, that I am not afraid of their letting things go wrong to any length in any cause." The people may be misled or deceived for a time, but where the avenues of truth are open there men will learn to reject what is false and harmful. "Where the people are well-informed, they can be trusted with their own government; whenever things get so far wrong as to attract their notice, they may be relied on to set them to rights."

One of the basic needs of a democratic society, therefore, was popular education. Tyranny, Jefferson knew, had always battened upon ignorance. Where darkness reigned there men were not free. Only the full light of learning could dispel superstition and liberate the human mind for self-government. A democratic society without popular education was, indeed, unthinkable. "If a nation expects to be ignorant and free . . . , it expects what never was and never will be." Jefferson favored universal popular education not only for the sake of perpetuating democracy and making it work, but also because of the happiness that men could derive from a widened mental horizon. "In the present spirit of extending to the great mass of mankind the blessing of instruction, I see a prospect of great advancement in the happiness of the human race."

For the same reason Jefferson advocated an untrammeled press. If a democracy needed citizens who could read, it followed that they had to be free in their reading. Censorship of any kind would negate the very spirit of democracy by substituting the tyranny over the mind for the despotism over the body. Moreover, since the essence of democracy was the right of minorities to be heard, the principle of censorship would supply the majority with a tyrannical weapon. "Our liberty," Jefferson said, "depends on the freedom of the press, and that cannot be limited without being lost." And although Jefferson was the victim of unrestrained abuse on the part of the newspapers—most of them were venal—he felt that the press must be protected at all costs. During his first administration he said of the rabid newspapers: "I shall protect them in the right of lying and calumniating."

The same principle applied also to books. Jefferson said that if the facts in a book were false they should be disproved, and if the reasoning was fallacious it should be refuted. "But, for God's sake, let us freely hear both sides." Unpopular ideas must be given a hearing and criticism encouraged. Without unhampered criticism of public figures and public policy, a democracy would soon deteriorate. "To demand the censors [critics] of public measures to be given up for punishment is to renew the demand of the wolves in the fable that the sheep should give up their dogs as hostages of the peace and confidence established between them."*

A democracy where men were free to think and say what they pleased also implied freedom of conscience. To Jefferson ecclesiastical tyranny was even more abhorrent than political despotism. Religious fanaticism, he was well aware, had caused bloodshed and suffering in the past. In his *Notes on*

* To Giles, December 17, 1794; MS, N. Y. Pub. Lib., MS, I, 152.

Virginia Jefferson wrote: "Millions of innocent men, women and children, since the introduction of Christianity, have been burnt, tortured, fined, imprisoned; yet we have not advanced one inch towards uniformity." Since religious uniformity was neither obtainable nor desirable, it was wise policy to give up the attempt altogether. Let each man worship as he please, or not worship as he please. Religion, Jefferson held, was a "matter between every man and his maker, in which no other, and far less the public had a right to intermeddle." Jefferson himself was no churchman, and he disliked creeds, but he held fast to the moral principles of Jesus.

To give the state power to prescribe the religion of the citizens was as intolerable as the principle of punishing people for their beliefs. One of the lasting achievements of the American Revolution was religious toleration, and all his life Jefferson took pride in his epoch-making Act for Establishing Religious Freedom which was passed by the Virginia Assembly in 1786. This Act, drafted by Jefferson, starts out with the lofty principle, "Well aware that Almighty God hath created the mind free," and concludes with the warning that any restrictions on conscience must be regarded as an "infringement of natural right." In Jefferson's humanistic philosophy religious toleration was a prime need not only for its own sake but for the preservation of democratic society. He knew the cruelty inherent in religious intolerance and the formidableness of the tyranny when a State joined forces with a dominant Church. Such a "loathsome combination of Church and State," as Jefferson called it, had in the past wrought havoc with human society and it must not be permitted to do so in America. "In every country and in every age, the priest has been hostile to liberty. He is always in alliance with the despot, abetting his abuses in return for protection of his own." In America men must be free in body as well as in mind, and no person or law should have the right to tell them what to believe. Jefferson stated this principle of toleration with striking bluntness when he said: "It does me no injury for my neighbor to say there are twenty gods, or no God. It neither picks my pocket nor breaks my leg."

Jefferson's devotion to American democracy led him to the principle of uncompromising isolation in the sphere of international politics. His bitter experiences could lead to no other course. It will be remembered that his most active years in politics coincided with one of Europe's periodic upheavals. When Jefferson was Secretary of State under President

Washington, the French were decapitating their monarchs and thereby inviting foreign war. When Jefferson was Vice-President of the United States, Bonaparte was beginning to win those victories that were paving the way for his dictatorship of Europe. When Jefferson was President of the United States, he faced a world trampled by Napoleon on land and ravaged by the British on sea. For more than two decades, during most of which time Jefferson was in office, the world knew no peace. Jefferson viewed the international violence and bloodshed with something close to despair. "In the whole animal kingdom," he wrote bitterly to his friend Madison, "I recollect no family but man, steadily and systematically employed in the destruction of itself." And more than one hundred and thirty years ago he uttered a plaint that could, with even greater justice, be spoken to-day: "The moral principles and conventional usages which have heretofore been the bond of civilized nations . . . have now given way to force, the law of Barbarians, and the nineteenth century dawns with the Vandalism of the fifth."

The combatants ruthlessly violated American rights and American shipping. What was the United States to do? Go to war? Such a remedy, in Jefferson's view, was as bad as the disease. "I love peace," he wrote, "and I am anxious that we should give the world still another useful lesson, by showing to them other modes of punishing injuries than by war, which is as much a punishment to the punisher as to the sufferer." This "other mode" was to cut off all communications with the belligerents, to have no commercial dealings with any aggressor, and not to permit their quarrels to disrupt America's free institutions. America's unique position in a chaotic world was stated by Jefferson in words which still have the force of relevance to-day:

"Our difficulties are indeed great, if we consider ourselves alone. But when viewed in comparison to those of Europe, they are the joys of Paradise. . . . The destinies have placed our portion of existence amidst such scenes of tumult and outrage, as no other period, within our knowledge, has presented. . . . A conqueror roaming over the earth with havoc and destruction. . . . Indeed . . . , ours is a bed of roses. And the system of government which shall keep us afloat amidst the wreck of the world, will be immortalized in history. We have, to be sure, our petty squabbles and heart burnings, and we have something of the blue devils at times. . . . But happily for us, the Mammoth cannot swim, nor the

Leviathan move on dry land; and if we will keep out of their way, they cannot get at us."

Jefferson's policy was not only to keep out of the way of the European "lions and tigers," as he called them, but, equally important, to keep them out of America's way. He hoped that some means could be found to establish a line of demarcation in mid-ocean, so as to separate the two hemispheres forever. He saw the future of the American continent as a home of freedom and peace, and was anxious to keep war-torn Europe from infecting the Western hemisphere with its madness. Jefferson's correspondence with his disciple President Monroe shows how deeply he felt on this subject of isolation—perhaps insulation would be a better word—which came to be embodied in the "Monroe Doctrine." One of Jefferson's letters to Monroe elucidates this doctrine:

"I have ever deemed it fundamental for the United States never to take active part in the quarrels of Europe. Their political interests are entirely distinct from ours. Their mutual jealousies, their balance of power, their complicated alliances, their forms and principles of government, are all foreign to us. They are nations of eternal war. All their energies are expended in the destruction of the labor, property and lives of their people. On our part, never had a people so favorable a chance of trying the opposite system, of peace and fraternity with mankind, and the direction of all our means and faculties to the purposes of improvement instead of destruction. . . . Of the brethren of our own hemisphere, none are yet, or for an age to come will be, in a shape, condition, or disposition to war against us. And the foothold which the nations of Europe had in either America, is slipping from under them, so that we shall soon be rid of their neighborhood."

The notion of isolation in the sphere of international politics also carried over into the realm of economic activity. A farmer and the son of a farmer, Jefferson had a distrust of cities and commercial classes. He could never overcome his bias against an urban economy and an urban civilization. Country people were preferable to city dwellers, Jefferson believed, essentially because land ownership gave them a sense of freedom and independence.

Fearing urbanization and the consequent deterioration of democratic virtue, Jefferson was anxious to see the United States remain an agricultural society, growing its own foodstuffs but not producing its own manufactured products. "For the general operations of manufacture, let our workshops remain in Europe." Let Europe keep its proletariat and its slum cities, while America remains an agricultural democracy with open spaces. Contact with Europe should be limited to a mere exchange of agricultural commodities for manufactured articles.

Conditions have changed since Jefferson's time. Modern technology has conquered space, and the United States can no longer view her isolation with complacency. An even profounder change has taken place in the American economy. From an agricultural nation of some 5,000,000 in 1800, the United States has become a highly industrialized power with a population of 130,000,000, the majority of which live in cities and not on the land. Industrialized centers have given rise to complex problems and even sharp social conflicts, but they also have helped to redefine our democracy. Jefferson would have been surprised, and probably delighted, to know that American city-dwellers have shown themselves, by and large, as capable of the democratic life as were the country-folk of his time.

Jefferson knew that nothing in human society was permanent or immutable. In a crisis, where the well-being of his fellow citizens was involved, Jefferson himself ignored theory. All lovers of a progressive democracy will applaud the following words, written by Jefferson in 1816:

"Some men look at constitutions with sanctimonious reverence and deem them like the ark of the covenant, too sacred to be touched. They ascribe to the men of the preceding age a wisdom more than human, and suppose what they did to be beyond amendment. . . . I am certainly not an advocate for frequent and untried changes in laws and constitutions. . . . But I know also that laws and constitutions must go hand in hand with the progress of the human mind. . . . As new discoveries are made, new truths disclosed, and manners and opinions change with the change of circumstances, institutions must advance also, and keep pace with the times. We might as well require a man to wear still the coat which fitted him when a boy, as civilized society to remain ever under the regimen of their barbarous ancestors. . . . Each generation . . . has a right to choose for itself the form of government it believes the most promotive of its own happiness."

The modern trend is in the direction of a greater concentration of power in the hands of government. The problem of individual freedom within the framework of a more or less regulated economy will have to be fought out in our age, just as the question of political liberty and the free market were the issues in Jefferson's day. We will have to proceed along democratic lines, for such is our tradition and, one hopes, our wisdom.

Jefferson felt that without liberty, life was not worth living. Americans know that the democratic ideal requires faith and that the democratic way of life takes courage. In the difficult years that undoubtedly lie ahead, Americans will have to gather all their moral forces for the preservation of their way of life, their liberties, and their opportunities. And Jefferson, the democratic seer who had formulated the basic principles that govern the relations of the free citizens to his chosen government, will serve as a wise guide and a steady beacon, for he had himself struggled with the problems that perplex our civilization and had the indomitable courage to believe that "light and liberty are on steady advance."

The editor hopes that this book, containing the essentials of Jefferson's political and social thought, will add its contribution to an understanding and a new appreciation of American democracy. This is not an anthology, but a fairly integrated book containing statements of principles and arranged in logical sequence. The selections are taken from Jefferson's published writings and from the typescripts in the New York Public Library Manuscript Room.* No interpolations have been made by the editor, who has confined his editorial work to an arrangement of the materials under subject headings and occasional omissions (indicated by three dots) of words or sentences that seem irrelevant to the main argument. Spelling and structure are left as in the original. The editor has of course exercised discretion in the selection of materials, especially in order to avoid repetition. Those who will want Jefferson's ideas in a nutshell, so to speak, can consult Appendix I, which contains axioms and dicta arranged alphabetically by subject matter.

The editor wishes to take this opportunity to thank Mrs. Eleanor Berman and Miss Esther Davidson for their help in the preparation of the manuscript, and Mr. Francis G. Wickware for his encouragement.

SAUL K. PADOVER

* The Library of Congress contains the bulk of Jefferson's manuscript materials, but the cream has been skimmed and can be found in published form.

CHAPTER I

NATURAL RIGHTS OF MAN

These truths are self-evident—
Declaration of Independence, 1776

WE HOLD these truths to be self-evident:
  that all men are created equal;
  that they are endowed by their Creator with inherent and*
unalienable rights;
  that among these are life, liberty, and the pursuit of happiness;
  that to secure these rights, governments are instituted among men, deriving their just powers from the consent of the governed;
  that whenever any form of government becomes destructive of these ends, it is the right of the people to alter or to abolish it, and to institute new government, laying its foundation on such principles and organizing its powers in such form, as to them shall seem most likely to effect their safety and happiness.†

Man is born free
To—(?), 1813: N. Y. Pub. Lib., MS, IV, 193

We acknowledge that our children are born free; that that freedom is the gift of nature, and not of him who begot them; that they [are] under our care during infancy, and therefore of necessity under a duly tempered authority, that care is confided to us to be exercised for the preservation and good of the child only. . . . As he was never the property of his father so, when adult, he is *sui juris,* entitled himself to the use of his own limbs, and the fruits of his own exertions.

---

* Congress deleted "inherent and" and substituted "certain."

† "When forced, therefore, to resort to arms for redress, an appeal to the tribunal of the world was deemed proper for our justification. This was the object of the Declaration of Independence. Not to find out new principles, or new arguments, never before thought of, not merely to say things which had never been said before; but to place before mankind the common sense of the subject, in terms so plain and firm as to command their assent, and to justify ourselves in the independent stand we are compelled to take. Neither aiming at originality of principle or sentiment, nor yet copied from any particular and previous writing, it was intended to be an expression of the American mind, and to give to that expression the proper tone and spirit called for by the occasion." (*To Henry Lee, 1825.*)

Right to throw off a despotic government
Declaration of Independence, 1776

Prudence, indeed, will dictate that Governments long established should not be changed for light and transient causes; and accordingly all experience hath shown, that mankind are more disposed to suffer, while evils are sufferable, than to right themselves by abolishing the forms to which they are accustomed. But when a long train of abuses and usurpations pursuing invariably the same Object, evinces a design to reduce them under absolute Despotism, it is their right, it is their duty, to throw off such Government, and to provide new Guards for their future security.

Right to individual liberty
To Monroe, 1782

If we are made in some degree for others, yet, in a greater, are we made for ourselves. It were contrary to feeling, and indeed ridiculous to suppose that a man had less rights in himself than one of his neighbors, or indeed all of them put together. This would be slavery, and not that liberty which the bill of rights has made inviolable, and for the preservation of which our government has been charged. Nothing could so completely divest us of that liberty as the establishment of the opinion, that the State has a perpetual right to the services of all its members. This, to men of certain ways of thinking, would be to annihilate the blessings of existence, and to contradict the Giver of life, who gave it for happiness and not for wretchedness. And certainly, to such it were better that they had never been born.

Right to think and act freely
To Humphreys, 1789

There are rights which it is useless to surrender to the government, and which governments have yet always been found to invade. These are the rights of thinking, and publishing our thoughts by speaking or writing; the right of free commerce; the right of personal freedom. There are instruments for administering the government, so peculiarly trust-worthy, that we should never leave the legislature at liberty to change them. The new Constitution has secured these in the executive and legislative department; but not in the judiciary. It should have established trials by the people themselves, that is to say, by jury. There are instruments so dangerous to the rights of the nation, and which place them so totally at the mercy of their governors, that those governors, whether legislative or executive, should be restrained from keeping such instruments on foot, but in well-defined cases. Such an instrument is a standing army.

Right of self-government
Opinion . . . whether the seat of government shall be transferred to the Potomac, July 15, 1790

Every man, and every body of men on earth, possess the right of self-government. They receive it with their being from the hand of nature. Individuals exercise it by their single will; collections of men by that of their majority; for the law of the *majority* is the natural law of every society of men.

Right of free communication
To Monroe, 1797

A right of free correspondence between citizen and citizen, on their joint interests, whether public or private, and under whatsoever laws these interests arise . . . , is a natural right; it is not the gift of any municipal law, either of England, or Virginia, or of Congress; but in common with all our other natural rights, it is one of the objects for the protection of which society is formed, and municipal laws established.

One generation has no right to bind another
To J. W. Eppes, 1813

The earth belongs to the living, not to the dead. The will and the power of man expire with his life, by nature's law. Some societies give it an artificial continuance, for the encouragement of industry; some refuse it, as our aboriginal neighbors, whom we call barbarians. The generations of men may be considered as bodies or corporations. Each generation has the usufruct of the earth during the period of its continuance. When it ceases to exist, the usufruct passes on to the succeeding generation, free and unincumbered, and so on, successively, from one generation to another forever.

We may consider each generation as a distinct nation, with a right, by the will of its majority, to bind themselves, but none to bind the succeeding generation, more than the inhabitants of another country. Or the case may be likened to the ordinary one of a tenant for life, who may hypothecate the land for his debts, during the continuance of his usufruct; but at his death, the reversioner (who is also for life only) receives it exonerated from all burthen. The period of a generation, or the term of its life, is determined by the laws of mortality, which, varying a little only in different climates, offer a general average, to be found by observation. I turn, for instance, to Buffon's tables, of twenty-three thousand nine hundred and ninety-four deaths, and the ages at which they happened, and I find that of the numbers of all ages living at one moment, half will be dead in twenty-four years and eight months. But (leaving out minors, who have not the power of self-government) of the adults (of twenty-one years of age) living at one moment, a majority of whom act for the society, one half will be dead in eighteen years and eight months. At nineteen years then from the date of a contract, the majority of the contractors are dead, and their contract with them.

To Governor Plumer, 1816

The idea that institutions established for the use of the nation cannot be touched nor modified, even to make them answer their end, because of rights gratuitously supposed in those employed to manage them in trust for the public, may perhaps be a salutary provision against the abuses of a monarch, but is most absurd against the nation itself. Yet our lawyers and priests generally inculcate this doctrine, and suppose that preceding generations held the earth more freely than we do; had a right to impose laws on us, unalterable by ourselves, and that we, in like manner, can make laws and impose burthens on future generations, which they will have no right to alter; in fine, that the earth belongs to the dead and not the living.

To T. Earle, 1823

That our Creator made the earth for the use of the living and not of the dead; that those who exist not can have no use nor right in it, no authority or power over it; that one generation of men cannot foreclose or burthen its use to another, which comes to it in its own right and by the same divine beneficence; that a preceding generation cannot bind a succeeding one by its laws or contracts; these deriving their obligation from the will of the existing majority, and that majority being removed by death, another comes in its place with a will equally free to make its own laws and contracts; these are axioms so self-evident that no explanation can make them plainer.

Man is born with a moral instinct
To T. Law, 1814

Some men are born without the organs of sight, or of hearing, or without hands. Yet it would be wrong to say that man is born without these faculties, and sight, hearing, and hands may with truth enter into the general definition of man. The want or imperfection of the moral sense in some men, like the want or imperfection of the sense of sight and hearing in others, is no proof that it is a general characteristic of the species. When it is wanting, we endeavor to supply the defect by education, by appeals to reason and calculation, by presenting to the being so unhappily conformed, other motives to do good and to eschew evil, such as the love, or the hatred, or rejection of those among whom he lives, and whose society is necessary to his happiness and even existence; demonstrations by sound calculation that honesty promotes interest in the long run; the rewards and penalties established by the laws; and ultimately the prospects of a future state of retribution for the evil as well as the good done while here. These are the correctives which are supplied by education, and which exercise the functions of the moralist, the preacher, and legislator. . . .

Some have argued against the existence of a moral sense, by saying that if nature had given us such a sense . . . , then nature would also have designated, by some particular earmarks, the two sets of actions which are, in themselves, the one virtuous and the other vicious. Whereas, we find, in fact, that the same actions are deemed virtuous in one country and vicious in another. The answer is that nature has constituted *utility* to man the standard and best of virtue. Men living in different countries, under different circumstances, different habits and regimens, may have different utilities; the same act, therefore, may be useful, and consequently virtuous in one country which is injurious and vicious in another differently circumstanced. I sincerely, then, believe . . . in the general existence of a moral instinct. I think it the brightest gem with which the human character is studded, and the want of it as more degrading than the most hideous of the bodily deformities.

Natural limits of the laws
To F. W. Gilmer, 1816

Our legislators are not sufficiently apprized of the rightful limits of their power; that their true office is to declare and enforce only our natural rights and duties, and to take none of them from us. No man has a natural right to commit aggression on the equal rights of another; and this is all from which the laws ought to restrain him; every man is under the natural duty of contributing to the necessities of the society; and this is all the laws should enforce on him; and, no man having a natural right to be the judge between himself and another, it is his natural duty to submit to the umpirage of an impartial third. When the laws have declared and enforced all this, they have fulfilled their functions, and the idea is quite unfounded, that on entering into society we give up any natural right.

Summary of man's rights in society
To Dupont de Nemours, 1816

I believe . . . that morality, compassion, generosity, are innate elements of the human constitution; that there exists a right independent of force; that a right to property is founded in our natural wants, in the means with which we are endowed to satisfy these wants, and the right to what we acquire by those means without violating the similar rights of other sensible beings; that no one has a right to obstruct another, exercising his faculties innocently for the relief of sensibilities made a part of his nature; that justice is the fundamental law of society; that the majority, oppressing an individual, is guilty of a crime, abuses its strength, and by acting on the law of the strongest breaks up the foundations of society; that action by the citizens in person, in affairs within their reach and competence, and in all others by representatives, chosen immediately, and removable by themselves, constitutes the essence of a republic; that all governments are more or less republican in proportion as this principle enters more or less into their composition; and that a government by representation is capable of extension over a greater surface of country than one of any other form.

Hope
To Weightman, June 24, 1826

All eyes are opened, or opening, to the rights of man. The general spread of the light of science has already laid open to every view the palpable truth, that the mass of mankind has not been born with saddles on their backs, nor a favored few booted and spurred, ready to ride them legitimately, by the grace of God.

CHAPTER II

PRINCIPLES OF DEMOCRACY
CREDO

To Hartley, 1787

I HAVE no fear, but that the result of our experiment will be, that men may be trusted to govern themselves without a master. Could the contrary of this be proved, I should conclude, either that there is no God, or that he is a malevolent being.

I. ADVANTAGES OF DEMOCRACY

—and of revolution
To Madison, 1787

Societies exist under three forms, sufficiently distinguishable. 1. Without government, as among our Indians. 2. Under governments, wherein the will of every one has a just influence; as is the case in England, in a slight degree, and in our States, in a great one. 3. Under governments of force; as is the case in all other monarchies, and in most of the other republics. To have an idea of the curse of existence under these last, they must be seen. It is a government of wolves over sheep. It is a problem, not clear in my mind, that the first condition is not the best. But I believe it to be inconsistent with any great degree of population. The second state has a great deal of good in it. The mass of mankind under that, enjoys a precious degree of liberty and happiness. It has its evils, too; the principal of which is the turbulence to which it is subject. But weigh this against the oppressions of monarchy, and it becomes nothing. *Malo periculosam libertatem quam quietam servitutem.* Even this evil is productive of good. It prevents the degeneracy of government, and nourishes a general attention to the public affairs. I hold it, that a little rebellion, now and then, is a good thing, and as necessary in the political world as storms in the physical. Unsuccessful rebellions, indeed, generally establish the encroachments on the rights of the people, which have produced them. An observation of this truth should render honest republican governors so mild in their punishment of rebellions, as not to discourage them too much. It is a medicine necessary for the sound health of government.

To Wm. S. Smith, 1787

God forbid we should ever be twenty years without such a rebellion. The people cannot be all, and always, well informed. The part which is wrong will be discontented, in proportion to the importance of the facts they misconceive. If they remain quiet under such misconceptions, it is a lethargy, a forerunner of death to the public liberty. We have had thirteen States independent for eleven years. There has been one rebellion. That comes to one rebellion in a century and a half, for each State. What country before, ever existed a century and a half without a rebellion? And what country can preserve its liberties, if its rulers are not warned from time to time, that this people preserve the spirit of resistance? Let them take arms. The remedy is to set them right as to facts, pardon and pacify them. What signify a few lives lost in a century or two? The tree of liberty must be refreshed from time to time, with the blood of patriots and tyrants. It is its natural manure.

The French Revolution and the Terror
To Short, 1793

In the struggle which was necessary, many guilty persons fell without the forms of trial, and with them some innocent. These I deplore as much as any body, and shall deplore some of them to the day of my death. But I deplore them as I should have done had they fallen in battle. It was necessary to use the arm of the people, a machine not quite so blind as balls and bombs, but blind to a certain degree. A few of their cordial friends met at their hands the fate of enemies. But time and truth will rescue and embalm their memories, while their posterity will be enjoying that very liberty for which they would never have hesitated to offer up their lives. The liberty of the whole earth was depending on the issue of the contest, and was ever such a prize won with so little innocent blood? My own affections have been deeply wounded by some of the martyrs to this cause, but rather than it should have failed I would have seen half the earth desolated; were there but an

Adam and Eve left in every country, and left free, it would be better than as it now is.

The democratic revolution will ultimately win
To Adams, 1823

The generation which commences a revolution rarely completes it. Habituated from their infancy to passive submission of body and mind to their kings and priests, they are not qualified when called on to think and provide for themselves; and their inexperience, their ignorance and bigotry make them instruments often, in the hands of the Bonapartes and Iturbides, to defeat their own rights and purposes. This is the present situation of Europe and Spanish America. But it is not desperate. The light which has been shed on mankind by the art of printing, has eminently changed the condition of the world. As yet, that light has dawned on the middling classes only of the men in Europe. The kings and the rabble, of equal ignorance, have not yet received its rays; but it continues to spread, and while printing is preserved, it can no more recede than the sun return on his course. A first attempt to recover the right of self-government may fail, so may a second, a third, etc. But as a younger and more instructed race comes on, the sentiment becomes more and more intuitive, and a fourth, a fifth or some subsequent one of the ever renewed attempts will ultimately succeed.

In France, the first effort was defeated by Robespierre, the second by Bonaparte, the third by Louis XVIII and his holy allies: another is yet to come, and all Europe, Russia excepted, has caught the spirit; and all will attain representative government, more or less perfect. This is now well understood to be a necessary check on kings, whom they will probably think it more prudent to chain and tame, than to exterminate. To attain all this, however, rivers of blood must yet flow, and years of desolation pass over; yet the object is worth rivers of blood, and years of desolation.

Why the Greeks had no conception of popular government
To I. H. Tiffany, 1816

But so different was the style of society then and with those people [the Greeks in the time of Aristotle], from what it is now and with us, that I think little edification can be obtained from their writings on the subject of government. They had just ideas of the value of personal liberty, but none at all of the structure of government best calculated to preserve it. They knew no medium between a democracy (the only pure republic) and an abandonment of themselves to an aristocracy or a tyranny independent of the people. It seems not to have occurred that where the citizens cannot meet to transact their business in person, they alone have the right to choose the agents who shall transact it; and that in this way a republican, or popular government, of the second grade of purity, may be exercised over any extent of country.

The full experiment of government democratical, but representative, was and still is reserved for us. The idea (taken, indeed, from the little specimen formerly existing in the English constitution, but now lost) has been carried by us, more or less, into all our legislative and executive departments. . . . The introduction of this new principle of representative democracy has rendered useless almost everything written before on the structure of government; and, in a great measure, relieves our regret, if the political writings of Aristotle, or of any other ancient, have been lost. . . . My most earnest wish is to see the republican element of popular control pushed to the maximum of its practicable exercise. I shall then believe that our government may be pure and perpetual.

Rome had no democracy because the people were depraved
To Adams, 1819

And if Cæsar had been as virtuous as he was daring and sagacious, what could he, even in the plentitude of his usurped power, have done to lead his fellow citizens into good government? I do not say to *restore it,* because they never had it, from the rape of the Sabines to the ravages of the Cæsars. If their people indeed had been, like ourselves, enlightened, peaceable, and really free, the answer would be obvious. "Restore independence to all your foreign conquests, relieve Italy from the government of the rabble of Rome, consult it as a nation entitled to self-government, and do its will." But steeped in corruption, vice and venality, as the whole nation was (and nobody had done more than Cæsar to corrupt it), what could even Cicero, Cato, Brutus have done, had it been referred to them to establish a good government for their country? They had no ideas of government themselves, but of their degenerate Senate, nor the people of liberty, but of the factious opposition of their Tribunes. They had afterwards their Tituses, their Trajans, and Antoninuses, who had the will to make them happy, and the power to mould their government into a good and permanent form. But it would seem as if they could not see their way clearly to do it. No government can continue good, but under the control of the people; and their people were so demoralized and depraved, as to be incapable of exercising a wholesome control.

Democracy means stability;—despotism, insurrection
To Madison, 1787

I own, I am not a friend to a very energetic government. It is always oppressive. It places the governors indeed more at their ease, at the expense of the people. The late rebellion in Massachusetts has given more alarm, than I think it should have done. Calculate that one rebellion in thirteen States in the course of eleven years, is but one for each State in a century and a half. No country should be so long without one. Nor will any degree of power in the hands of government, prevent insurrections. In England, where the hand of power is heavier than with us, there are seldom half a dozen years without an insurrection. In France, where it is still heavier, but less despotic, as Montesquieu supposes, than in some other countries, and where there are always two or three hundred thousand men ready to crush insurrections, there have been three in the course of the three years I have been here, in every one of which greater numbers were engaged than in Massachusetts, and a great deal more blood was spilt. In Turkey, where the sole nod of the despot is death, insurrections are the events of every day. Compare again the ferocious depredations of their insurgents, with the order, the moderation and the almost self-extinguishment of ours. And say, finally, whether peace is best preserved by giving energy to the government, or information to the people. This last is the most certain, and the most legitimate engine of government. Educate and inform the whole mass of the people. Enable them to see that it is their interest to preserve peace and order, and they will preserve them. And it requires no very high degree of education to convince them of this. They are the only sure reliance for the preservation of our liberty. After all, it is my principle that the will of the majority should prevail. If they approve the proposed constitution in all its parts, I shall concur in it cheerfully, in hopes they will amend it, whenever they shall find it works wrong.

To De Meunier, 1786

It has been said, too, that our governments, both federal and particular, want energy; that it is difficult to restrain both individuals and States from committing wrong. This is true, and it is an inconvenience. On the other hand, that energy which absolute governments derive from an armed force, which is the effect of the bayonet constantly held at the breast of every citizen, and which resembles very much the stillness of the grave, must be admitted also to have its inconveniences. We weigh the two together, and like best to submit to the former. Compare the number of wrongs committed with impunity by citizens among us with those committed by the sovereign in other countries, and the last will be found most numerous, most oppressive on the mind, and most degrading of the dignity of man.

First Inaugural, March 4, 1801

I know, indeed, that some honest men fear that a republican government cannot be strong; that this government is not strong enough. But would the honest patriot, in the full tide of successful experiment, abandon a government which has so far kept us free and firm, on the theoretic and visionary fear that this government, the world's best hope, may by possibility want energy to preserve itself? I trust not. I believe this, on the contrary, the strongest government on earth. I believe it is the only one where every man, at the call of the laws, would fly to the standard of the law, and would meet invasions of the public order as his own personal concern. Sometimes it is said that man cannot be trusted with the government of himself. Can he, then, be trusted with the government of others? Or have we found angels in the forms of kings to govern him? Let his history answer this question.

Republic is paradise compared to monarchy
To Hawkins, 1787

And above all things, I am astonished at some people's considering a kingly government as a refuge. Advise such to read the fable of the frogs who solicited Jupiter for a king. If that does not put them to rights, send them to Europe, to see something of the trappings of monarchy, and I will undertake that every man shall go back thoroughly cured. If all the evils which can arise among us, from the republican form of government, from this day to the day of judgment, could be put into a scale against what this country suffers from its monarchical form in a week, or England in a month, the latter would preponderate. Consider the contents of the Red book in England, or the Almanac royale of France, and say what a people gain by monarchy. No race of kings has ever presented above one man of common sense in twenty generations. The best they can do is, to leave things to their ministers; and what are their ministers, but a committee, badly chosen? If the king ever meddles, it is to do harm.

To—(?), 1793

Should the present foment in Europe not produce republics everywhere, it will at least soften the monarchical governments by rendering monarchs amenable to punishment like other criminals, and doing away that rages of insolence and oppression, the inviolability of the King's person. We I hope shall adhere to our republican government, and keep it to its original principles by narrowly watching it.

Ours is a blessed government
To Rutledge, 1787

And we think ours a bad government. The only condition on earth to be compared with ours, in my opinion, is that of the Indian, where they have still less law than we. The European, are governments of kites over pigeons. The best schools for republicanism are London, Versailles, Madrid, Vienna, Berlin, etc.

To Monroe, 1785

I sincerely wish you may find it convenient to come here; the pleasure of the trip will be less than you expect, but the utility greater. It will make you adore your own country, its soil, its climate, its equality, liberty, laws, people, and manners. My God! how little do my countrymen know what precious blessings they are in possession of and which no other people on earth enjoy. I confess I had no idea of it myself. While we shall see multiplied instances of Europeans going to live in America, I will venture to say, no man now living will ever see an instance of an American removing to settle in Europe, and continuing there.

To Ramsay, 1787

I am sensible that there are defects in our federal government, yet they are so much lighter than those of monarchies, that I view them with much indulgence. I rely, too, on the good sense of the people for remedy, whereas the evils of monarchical government are beyond remedy. If any of our countrymen wish for a King, give them Aesop's fable of the frogs who asked a King; if this does not cure them, send them to Europe. They will go back good republicans.

European monarchs—fools and madmen
To J. Langdon, 1810

The practice of Kings marrying only in the families of Kings, has been that of Europe for some centuries. Now, take any race of animals, confine them in idleness and inaction, whether in a stye, a stable or a stateroom, pamper them with high diet, gratify all their sexual appetites, immerse them in sensualities, nourish their passions, let everything bend before them, and banish whatever might lead them to think, and in a few generations they become all body and no mind . . . Such is the regimen in raising Kings, and in this way they have gone on for centuries.

While in Europe, I often amused myself with contemplating the characters of the then reigning sovereigns . . . Louis XVI was a fool, of my own knowledge . . . The King of Spain [Charles IV] was a fool, and of Naples [Ferdinand IV] the same. They passed their lives in hunting, and despatch two couriers a week, one thousand miles, to let each other know what game they had killed the preceding days. The King of Sardinia [Victor Amadeus III] was a fool. All these were Bourbons. The queen of Portugal [the Mad Maria], a Braganza, was an idiot by nature. And so was the King of Denmark [Christian VII]. Their sons, as regents, exercised the powers of government. The King of Prussia [Frederick William II], successor to the great Frederick, was a mere hog in body as well as in mind. Gustavus [III] of Sweden, and Joseph [II] of Austria, were really crazy, and George [III] of England, you know, was in a straight waistcoat. There remained, then, none but old Catharine, who had been too lately picked up to have lost her common sense. . . . These animals had become without mind and powerless; and so will every hereditary monarch be after a few generations. . . . And so endeth the book of Kings, from all of whom the Lord deliver us.

To Humphreys, 1787

So much for the blessings of having Kings, and magistrates who would be Kings. From these events, our young Republic may learn useful lessons, never to call on foreign powers to settle their differences, to guard against hereditary magistrates, to prevent their citizens from becoming so established in wealth and power, as to be thought worthy of alliance by marriage with the nieces, sisters, &c., of Kings, and, in short, to besiege the throne of heaven with eternal prayers, to extirpate from creation this class of human lions, tigers, and mammoths called Kings; from whom, let him perish who does not say, "good Lord deliver us."

11. American Democracy

—a beacon to mankind
To Hunter, 1790

Convinced that the republican is the only form of government which is not eternally at open or secret war with the rights of mankind, my prayers and efforts shall be cordially distributed to the support of that we have so happily established. It is indeed an animating thought, that while we are securing the rights of ourselves and our posterity, we are pointing out the way to struggling nations, who wish like us to emerge from their tyrannies also.

To Rutledge, 1788

But my confidence is, that there will, for a long time, be virtue and good sense enough in our countrymen, to correct abuses. We can surely boast of having set the world a beautiful example of a government reformed by reason alone, without bloodshed. But the world is too far oppressed, to profit by the example. On this side of the Atlantic, the blood of the people is become an inheritance, and those who fatten on it, will not relinquish it easily.

To Governor Hall, 1802: N. Y. Pub. Lib., MS, II, 217-18

We have the same object, the success of representative government. Nor are we acting for ourselves alone, but for the whole human race. The event of our experiment is to show whether man can be trusted with self-government. The eyes of suffering humanity are fixed on us with anxiety as their only hope, and on such a theatre for such a cause we must suppress all smaller passions and local considerations. The leaders of federalism say that man can not be trusted with his own government.

To B. Galloway, 1812

I hope and firmly believe that the whole world will, sooner or later, feel benefit from the issue of our assertion of the rights of man. Although the horrors of the French revolution have damped for awhile the ardor of the patriots in every country, yet it is not extinguished—it will never die. The sense of right has been excited in every breast, and the spark will be rekindled by the very oppressions of that detestable tyranny employed to quench it. The errors of the honest patriots of France, and the crimes of her Dantons and Robespierres, will be forgotten in the more encouraging contemplation of our sober example, and steady march to our object. Hope will strengthen the presumption that what has been done once may be done again.

To R. Rush, 1820

We exist, and are quoted, as standing proofs that a government, so modelled as to rest continually on the will of the whole society, is a practicable government. Were we to break to pieces, it would damp the hopes and the efforts of the good, and give triumph to those of the bad through the whole enslaved world. As members, therefore, of the universal society of mankind, and standing in high and responsible relation with them, it is our sacred duty to suppress passions among ourselves, and not to blast the confidence we have inspired of proof that a government of reason is better than one of force.

Bright future of American democracy
First Inaugural, March 4, 1801

Let us, then, with courage and confidence pursue our own federal and republican principles, our attachment to our union and representative government. Kindly separated by nature and a wide ocean from the exterminating havoc of one quarter of the globe; too high-minded to endure the degradations of the others; possessing a chosen country, with room enough for our descendants to the hundredth and thousandth generation; entertaining a due sense of our equal right to the use of our own faculties, to the acquisitions of our industry, to honor and confidence from our fellow citizens, resulting not from birth but from our actions and their sense of them; enlightened by a benign religion, professed, indeed, and practiced in various forms, yet all of them including honesty, truth, temperance, gratitude, and the love of man; acknowledging and adoring an overruling Providence, which by all its dispensations proves that it delights in the happiness of man here and his greater happiness hereafter; with all these blessings, what more is necessary to make us a happy and prosperous people?

To De Marbois, 1817

I have much confidence that we shall proceed successfully for ages to come, and that, contrary to the principle of Montesquieu, it will be seen that the larger the extent of country, the more firm its republican structure, if founded, not on conquest, but in principles of compact and equality. My hope of its duration is built much on the enlargement of the resources of life going hand in hand with the enlargement of territory, and the belief that men are disposed to live honestly, if the means of doing so are open to them. With the consolation of this belief in the future result of our labors, I have that of other prophets who foretell distant events, that I shall not live to see it falsified. My theory has always been, that if we are to dream, the flatteries of hope are as cheap, and pleasanter than the gloom of despair.

Experience will prove the value of the American experiment
To D'Ivernois, 1795

I suspect that the doctrine, that small States alone are fitted to be republics, will be exploded by experience, with some other brilliant fallacies accredited by Montesquieu and other political writers. Perhaps it will be found, that to obtain a just republic (and it is to secure our just rights that we resort to government at all) it must be so extensive as that local egoisms may never reach its greater part; that on every particular question, a majority may be found in its councils free from particular interests, and giving, therefore, an uniform prevalence to the principles of justice. The smaller the societies, the more violent and convulsive their schisms.

We have chanced to live in an age which will probably be distinguished in history, for its experiments in government on a larger scale than has yet taken place. But we shall not live to see the result. The grosser absurdities, such as hereditary magistracies, we shall see exploded in our day, long experience having already pronounced condemnation against them. But what is to be the substitute? This our children or grandchildren will answer. We may be satisfied with the certain knowledge that none can ever be tried, so stupid, so unrighteous, so oppressive, so destructive of every end for which honest men enter into government, as that which their forefathers had established, and their fathers alone venture to tumble headlong. . . . It is unfortunate, that the efforts of mankind to recover the freedom of which they have been so long deprived, will be accompanied with violence, with errors, and even with crimes. But while we weep over the means, we must pray for the end.

Centralization would lead to despotism
To Gideon Granger, 1800

Our country is too large to have all its affairs directed by a single government. Public servants at such a distance and from under the eye of their constituents, must, from the circumstance of distance, be unable to administer and overlook all the details necessary for the good government of the citizens, and the same circumstance, by rendering detection impossible to their constituents, will invite the public agents to corruption, plunder and waste. And I do verily believe, that if the principle were to prevail, of a common law being in force in the United States . . . , it would become the most corrupt government on the earth. . . .

What an augmentation of the field for jobbing, speculating, plundering, office-building and office-hunting would be produced by an assumption of all the State powers into the hands of the General Government. The true theory of our Constitution is surely the wisest and best, that the States are independent as to everything within themselves, and united as to everything respecting foreign nations. Let the General Government be reduced to foreign concerns only, and let our affairs be disentangled from those of all other nations, except as to commerce, which the merchants will manage the better, the more they are left free to manage for themselves, and our General Government may be reduced to a very simple organization and a very unexpensive one; a few plain duties to be performed by a few servants.

III. Principles

Program of a democrat
  To Elbridge Gerry, 1799

I am for preserving to the States the powers not yielded by them to the Union, and to the legislature of the Union its constitutional share in the division of powers; and I am not for transferring all the powers of the States to the General Government, and all those of that government to the executive branch.

I am for a government rigorously frugal and simple, applying all the possible savings of the public revenue to the discharge of the national debt; and not for a multiplication of officers and salaries merely to make partisans, and for increasing, by every device, the public debt, on the principle of its being a public blessing.

I am for relying, for internal defence, on our militia solely, till actual invasion, and for such a naval force only as may protect our coasts and harbors from such depredations as we have experienced; and not for a standing army in time of peace, which may overawe the public sentiment; nor for a navy, which, by its own expenses and the eternal wars in which it will implicate us, will grind us with public burthens, and sink us under them.

I am for free commerce with all nations; political connection with none; and little or no diplomatic establishment. And I am not for linking ourselves by new treaties with the quarrels of Europe; entering that field of slaughter to preserve their balance, or joining in the confederacy of kings to war against the principles of liberty.

I am for freedom of religion, and against all maneuvres to bring about a legal ascendancy of one sect over another: for freedom of the press, and against all violations of the Constitution to silence by force and not by reason the complaints or criticisms, just or unjust, of our citizens against the conduct of their agents.

And I am for encouraging the progress of science in all its branches; and not for raising a hue and cry against the sacred name of philosophy; for awing the human mind by stories of raw-head and bloody bones to a distrust of its own vision, and to repose implicitly on that of others; to go backwards instead of forwards to look for improvement; to believe that government, religion, morality, and every other science were in the highest perfection in ages of the darkest ignorance, and that nothing can ever be devised more perfect than what was established by our forefathers.

To these I will add, that I was a sincere well-wisher to the success of the French revolution, and still wish it may end in the establishment of a free and well-ordered republic; but I have not been insensible under the atrocious depredations they have committed on our commerce.

The first object of my heart is my own country. In that is embarked my family, my fortune, and my own existence. I have not one farthing of interest, no one fibre of attachment out of it, nor a single motive of preference of any one nation to another, but in proportion as they are more or less friendly to us.

First Inaugural, March 4, 1801

About to enter, fellow citizens, on the exercise of duties which comprehend everything dear and valuable to you, it is proper that you should understand what I deem the essential principles of our government, and consequently those which ought to shape its administration. I will compress them within the narrowest compass they will bear, stating the general principle, but not all its limitations.

Equal and exact justice to all men, of whatever state or persuasion, religious or political;

peace, commerce, and honest friendship, with all nations—entangling alliances with none;

the support of the state governments in all their rights, as the most competent administrations for our domestic concerns and the surest bulwarks against anti-republican tendencies;

the preservation of the general government in its whole constitutional vigor, as the sheet anchor of our peace at home and safety abroad;

a jealous care of the right of election by the people—a mild and safe corrective of abuses which are lopped by the sword of the revolution where peaceable remedies are unprovided;

absolute acquiescence in the decisions of the majority—the vital principle of republics, from which there is no appeal but to force, the vital principle and immediate parent of despotism;

a well-disciplined militia—our best reliance in peace and for the first moments of war, till regulars may relieve them;

the supremacy of the civil over the military authority;

economy in the public expense, that labor may be lightly burdened;

the honest payment of our debts and sacred preservation of the public faith;

encouragement of agriculture, and of commerce as its handmaid;

the diffusion of information and the arraignment of all abuses at the bar of public reason;

freedom of religion;

freedom of the press;

freedom of person under the protection of the *habeas corpus;*

and trial by jury impartially selected—

these principles form the bright constellation which has gone before us, and guided our steps through an age of revolution and reformation. The wisdom of our sages and the blood of our heroes have been devoted to their attainment. They should be the creed of our political faith—the text of civil instruction—the touchstone by which to try the services of those we trust; and should we wander from them in moments of error or alarm, let us hasten to retrace our steps and to regain the road which alone leads to peace, liberty and safety.

All power is inherent in the people
To J. Cartwright, 1824

Hume, the great apostle of toryism, says . . . "It is belied by all history and experience that *the people are the origin of all just power.*" And where else will this degenerate son of science, this traitor to his fellow men, find the origin of *just* powers, if not in the majority of the society? Will it be in the minority? Or in an individual of that minority?

Our Revolution commenced on more favorable ground. It presented us an album on which we were free to write what we pleased. We had no occasion to search into musty records, to hunt up royal parchments, or to investigate the laws and institutions of a semi-barbarous ancestry. We appealed to those of nature. . . . We had never been permitted to exercise self-government. When forced to assume it, we were novices in its science. . . . We established, however, some, although not all its important principles. The constitutions of most of our States assert that all power is inherent in the people; that they may exercise it by themselves in all cases to which they think themselves competent . . . ; that they are entitled to freedom of person, freedom of religion, freedom of property, freedom of the press.

The minority has equal rights with the majority
First Inaugural, March 4, 1801

All, too, will bear in mind this sacred principle, that though the will of the majority is in all cases to prevail, that will, to be rightful, must be reasonable; that the minority possess their equal rights, which equal laws must protect, and to violate which would be oppression. Let us, then, fellow citizens, unite with one heart and one mind. Let us restore to social intercourse that harmony and affection without which liberty and even life itself are but dreary things. And let us reflect that having banished from our land that religious intolerance under which mankind so long bled and suffered, we have yet gained little if we countenance a political intolerance as despotic, as wicked, and capable of as bitter and bloody persecutions.

The law of the majority is sacred
To Baron von Humboldt, 1817

The first principle of republicanism is, that the *lex-majoris partis** is the fundamental law of every society of individuals of equal rights; to consider the will of the society enounced by the majority of a single vote, as sacred as if unanimous, is the first of all lessons in importance, yet the last which is thoroughly learnt. This law once disregarded, no other remains but that of force, which ends necessarily in military despotism. This has been the history of the French revolution.

True Principles
To S. Kercheval, 1816

Only lay down true principles, and adhere to them inflexibly. Do not be frightened into their surrender by the alarms of the timid, or the croakings of wealth against the ascendancy of the people. If experience be called for, appeal to that of our fifteen or twenty governments for forty years, and show me where the people have done half the mischief in these forty years, that a single despot would have done in a single year; or show half the riots and rebellions, the crimes and the punishments, which have taken place in any single nation, under kingly government, during the same period. The true foundation of republican government is the equal

* The law of the majority.

right of every citizen, in his person and property, and in their management. Try by this, as a tally, every provision of our constitution, and see if it hangs directly on the will of the people. Reduce your legislature to a convenient number for full, but orderly discussion. Let every man who fights or pays, exercise his just and equal right in their election. Submit them to approbation or rejection at short intervals. Let the executive be chosen in the same way, and for the same term, by those whose agent he is to be; and leave no screen of a council behind which to skulk from responsibility.

To Dickinson, 1801: N. Y. Pub. Lib., MS, II, 47

My principles, and those always received by the republicans, do not admit the removing of any person from office merely for a difference of political opinion. Malversations in office, and the exerting official influence to control the freedom of election are good causes for removal.

To G. Granger, 1801: N. Y. Pub. Lib., MS, II, 73

To bear up against this (formidable phalanx opposed to the republican features of our constitution), the talents and virtue of our country must be formed into a phalanx also. My wish is to collect in a mass round the administration all the abilities and respectability.... To give none of the (offices) to secondary characters. Good principles, wisely and honestly administered cannot fail to attach our fellow citizens to the order of things which we espoused.

To Dr. Walter Jones, 1801

I am sensible how far I ... fall short of effecting all the reformation which reason would suggest, and experience approve, were I free to do whatever I thought best; but when we reflect how difficult it is to move or inflect the great machine of society, how impossible to advance the notions of a whole people suddenly to ideal right, we see the wisdom of Solon's remark, that no more good must be attempted than the nation can bear.

To Nathaniel Niles, 1801

The late chapter of our history furnishes a lesson to man perfectly new. The times have been awful, but they have proved an useful truth, that the good citizen must never despair of the commonwealth. How many good men abandoned the deck, and gave up the vessel as lost. It furnishes a new proof of the falsehood of Montesquieu's doctrine, that a republic can be preserved only in a small territory. The reverse is the truth. Had our territory been even a third only of what it is, we were gone. But while frenzy and delusion like an epidemic, gained certain parts, the residue remained sound and untouched, and held on till their brethren could recover from the temporary delusion.

The American people are masters of their own destiny
To Dupont de Nemours, 1816

We of the United States, you know, are constitutionally and conscientiously democrats. We consider society as one of the natural wants with which man has been created; that he has been endowed with faculties and qualities to effect its satisfaction by concurrence of others having the same want; that when, by the exercise of these faculties, he has procured a state of society, it is one of his acquisitions which he has a right to regulate and control, jointly indeed with all those who have concurred in the procurement, whom he cannot exclude from its use or direction more than they him.

We think experience has proved it safer, for the mass of individuals composing the society, to reserve to themselves personally the exercise of all rightful powers to which they are competent, and to delegate those to which they are not competent to deputies named, and removable for unfaithful conduct, by themselves immediately. Hence with us, the people (by which is meant the mass of individuals composing the society) being competent to judge of the facts occurring in ordinary life, they have retained the functions of judges of facts, under the name of jurors; but being unqualified for the management of affairs requiring intelligence above the common level, yet competent judges of human character, they chose, for their management, representatives, some by themselves immediately, others by electors chosen by themselves . . .

We both consider the people as our children, and love them with parental affection. But you love them as infants whom you are afraid to trust without nurses; and I as adults whom I freely leave to self-government.

Basic rights of American citizens
To Coray, 1823

I have stated that the constitutions of our several States vary more or less in some particulars. But there are certain principles in which all agree, and which all cherish as vitally essential to the protection of life, liberty, property, and safety of the citizen.

1. Freedom of religion, restricted only from *acts* of trespass on that of others.

2. Freedom of person, securing every one from imprisonment, or other bodily restraint, but by the laws of the land. This is effected by the well-known law of *habeas corpus*.

3. Trial by jury, the best of all safe-guards for the person, the property, and the fame of every individual.

4. The exclusive right of legislation and taxation in the representatives of the people.

5. Freedom of the press, subject only to liability for personal injuries. This formidable censor of the public functionaries, by arraigning them at the tribunal of public opinion, produces reform peaceably, which must otherwise be done by revolution. It is also the best instrument for enlightening the mind of man, and improving him as a rational, moral, and social being.

Democratic public morality
To Madison, 1789

To say, in excuse, that gratitude is never to enter into the motives of national conduct, is to revive a principle which has been buried for centuries with its kindred principles of the lawfulness of assassination, poison, perjury, &c. All of these were legitimate principles in the dark ages which intervened between ancient and modern civilization, but exploded and held in just horror in the eighteenth century. I know but one code of morality for men, whether acting singly or collectively. He who says I will be a rogue when I act in company with a hundred others, but an honest man when I act alone, will be believed in the former assertion, but not in the latter. I would say with the poet, *"hic niger est, hunc tu Romane cavato."* If the morality of one man produces a just line of conduct in him, acting individually, why should not the morality of one hundred men produce a just line of conduct in them, acting together?

Freedom of discussion
To Benjamin Waring, 1801

In every country where man is free to think and to speak, differences of opinion will arise from difference of perception, and the imperfection of reason; but these differences when permitted, as in this happy country, to purify themselves by free discussion, are but as passing clouds overspreading our land transiently, and leaving our horizon more bright and serene. That love of order and obedience to the laws, which so remarkably characterize the citizens of the United States, are sure pledges of internal tranquillity; and the elective franchise, if guarded as the act of our safety, will peaceably dissipate all combinations to subvert a Constitution dictated by the wisdom, and resting on the will of the people. That will is the only legitimate foundation of any government.

Universal suffrage
To J. Moor, 1800

My opinion has always been in favor of [a general suffrage]. Still I find very honest men who, thinking the possession of some property necessary to give due independence of mind, are for restraining the elective franchise to property. I believe we may lessen the danger of buying and selling votes, by making the number of voters too great for any means of purchase. I may further say that I have not observed men's honesty to increase with their riches.

To M. Page, 1795

I do not believe with the Rochefoucaulds and Montaignes that fourteen out of fifteen men are rogues.... But I have always found that rogues would be uppermost... for those who, rising above the swinish multitude, always contrive to nestle themselves into the places of power and profit. These rogues set out with stealing the people's good opinion, and then steal from them the right of withdrawing it, by contriving laws and associations against the power of the people themselves.

A sense of justice
To F. W. Gilmer, 1816

Man was created for social intercourse; but social intercourse cannot be maintained without a sense of justice; then man must have been created with a sense of justice. There is an error into which most of the speculators on government have fallen, and which the well-known state of society of our Indians ought, before now, to have corrected. In their hypothesis of the origin of government, they suppose it to have commenced in the patriarchal or monarchical form. Our Indians are evidently in that state of nature which has passed the association of a single family; and not yet submitted to the authority of positive laws, or of any acknowledged magistrate. Every man, with them, is perfectly free to follow his own inclinations. But if, in doing this, he violates the rights of another, if the case be slight, he is punished by the disesteem of his society, or as we say, by public opinion; if serious, he is tomahawked as a dangerous enemy. Their leaders conduct them by the influence of their character only; and they follow, or not, as they please, him of whose character for wisdom or war they have the highest opinion.

The less government the better
Notes on Virginia, Query 11 (1787, revised ed.)

[The Indians] separated into so many little societies..., never having submitted themselves to any laws, any coercive power, any shadow of government. Their only controls are their manners, and that moral sense of right and wrong, which, like the sense of tasting and feeling in every man, makes a part of his nature. An offence against these is punished by contempt, by exclusion from society.... Imperfect as this species of coercion may seem, crimes are very rare among them; insomuch that were it made a question, whether no law, as among the savage Americans, or too much law, as among the civilized Europeans, submits man to the greatest evil, one who has seen both conditions of existence would pronounce it to the last; and that the sheep are happier of themselves, than under care of the wolves. It will be said, the great societies cannot exist without government. The savages, therefore, break them into small ones.

IV. Republicanism

What is a Republic?
To J. Taylor, 1816

It must be acknowledged that the term *republic* is of very vague application in every language. Witness the self-styled republics of Holland, Switzerland, Genoa, Venice, Poland. Were I to assign to this term a precise and definite idea, I would say, purely and simply, it means a government by its citizens in mass, acting directly and personally, according to rules established by the majority; and that every other government is more or less republican, in proportion as it has in its composition more or less of this ingredient of the direct action of the citizens. Such a government is evidently restrained to very narrow limits of space and population. I doubt if it would be practicable beyond the extent of a New England township.

The first shade from this pure element, which, like that of pure vital air, cannot sustain life of itself, would be where the powers of the government, being divided, should be exercised each by representatives chosen either *pro hac vice,* or for such short terms as should render secure the duty of expressing the will of their constituents. This I should consider as the nearest approach to a pure republic, which is practicable on a large scale of country or population. And we have examples of it in some of our State constitutions, which, if not poisoned by priest-craft, would prove its excellence over all mixtures with other elements; and, with only equal doses of poison, would still be the best.

Other shades of republicanism may be found in other forms of government, where the executive, judiciary and legislative functions, and the different branches of the latter, are chosen by the people more or less directly, for longer terms of years, or for life, or made hereditary; or where there are mixtures of authorities, some dependent on, and others independent of the people. The further the departure from direct and constant control by the citizens, the less has the government of the ingredient of republicanism; evidently none where the authorities are hereditary, as in France, Venice, etc., or self-chosen, as in Holland; and little, where for life, in proportion as the life continues in being after the act of election.

The purest republican feature in the government of our own State, is the House of Representatives. The Senate is equally so the first year, less the second, and so on. The Executive still less, because not chosen by the people directly. The Judiciary seriously anti-republican, because for life; and the national arm wielded, as you observe, by military leaders, irresponsible but to themselves. Add to this the vicious constitution of our county courts (to whom the justice, the executive administration, the taxation, the police, the military appointments of the county, and nearly all our daily concerns are confided), self-appointed, self-continued, holding their authorities for life, and with an impossibility of breaking in on the perpetual succession of any faction once possessed of the bench. They are in truth, the executive, the judiciary, and the military of their respective counties, and the sum of the counties makes the State. And add, also, that one half of our brethren who fight and pay taxes, are excluded, like Helots, from the rights of representation, as if society were instituted for the soil, and not for the men inhabiting it; or one half of these could dispose of the rights and the will of the other half, without their consent.

'What constitutes a State?
Not high-raised battlements, or labor'd mound,
    Thick wall, or moated gate;
Not cities proud, with spires and turrets crown'd;
    No: men, high minded men;
    Men, who their duties know;
But know their rights; and knowing, dare maintain.
    These constitute a State.'

Are the American governments republican?
To J. Taylor, 1816

If, then, the control of the people over the organs of their government be the measure of its republicanism, and I confess I know no other measure, it must be agreed that our governments have much less of republicanism than ought to have been expected; in other words, that the people have less regular control over their agents, than their rights and their interests require. And this I ascribe, not to any want of republican dispositions in those who formed these constitutions, but a submission of true principle to European authorities, to speculators on government, whose fears of the people have been inspired by the populace of their own great cities, and were unjustly entertained against the independent, the happy, and therefore orderly citizens of the United States.

Much I apprehend that the golden moment is past for reforming these heresies. The functionaries of public power rarely strengthen in their dispositions to abridge it, and an unorganized call for timely amendment is not likely to prevail against an organized opposition to it. We are always told that things are going on well; why change them? *"Chi sta bene, no si muove,"* said the Italian, "let him who stands well, stand still." This is true; and I verily believe they would go on well with us under an absolute monarch, while our present character remains, of order, industry and love of peace, and restrained, as he would be, by the proper spirit of the people. But it is while it remains such, we should provide against the consequences of its deterioration. And let us rest in the hope that it will yet be done, and spare ourselves the pain of evils which may never happen.

On this view of the import of the term *republic,* instead of saying, as has been said, "that it may mean anything or nothing," we may say with truth and meaning, that governments are more or less republican, as they have more or less of the element of popular election and control in their composition; and believing, as I do, that the mass of the citizens is the safest depository of their own rights, and especially, that the evils flowing from the duperies of the people, are less injurious than those from the egoism of their agents, I am a friend to that composition of government which has in it the most of this ingredient.

V. POLITICAL PARTIES

Aristocrats and democrats
To H. Lee, 1824

Men by their constitution are naturally divided into two parties. 1. Those who fear and distrust the people, and wish to draw all powers from them into the hands of the higher classes. 2dly those who identify themselves with the people, have confidence in them, cherish and consider them as the most honest and safe, although not the most wise depository of the public interests. In every country these two parties exist, and in every one where they are free to think, speak, and write, they will declare themselves. Call them therefore liberals and serviles, Jacobins and Ultras, Whigs and Tories, republicans and federalists, they are the same parties still and pursue the same object. The last appellation of aristocrats and democrats is the true one expressing the essence of all.

Political parties are essential to a democracy
To J. Taylor, 1798

In every free and deliberating society, there must, from the nature of man, be opposite parties, and violent dissensions and discords; and one of these, for the most part, must prevail over the other for a longer or shorter time. Perhaps this party division is necessary to induce each to watch and relate to the people the proceedings of the other. But if on a temporary superiority of the one party, the other is to resort to a scission of the Union, no federal government can ever exist.

If to rid ourselves of the present rule of Massachusetts and Connecticut, we break the Union, will the evil stop there? Suppose the New England States alone cut off, will our nature be changed? Are we not men still to the south of that, and with all the passions of men? Immediately, we shall see a Pennsylvania and a Virginia party arise in the residuary confederacy, and the public mind will be distracted with the same party spirit. What a game too will the one party have in their hands, by eternally threatening the other that unless they do so and so, they will join their northern neighbors. . . .

Seeing, therefore, that an association of men who will not quarrel with one another is a thing which never yet existed, from the greatest confederacy of nations down to a town meeting or a vestry; seeing that we must have somebody to quarrel with, I had rather keep our New England associates for that purpose, than to see our bickerings transferred to others.

America's two political parties
To John Wise, 1798

Two political Sects have arisen within the United States; the one believing that the Executive is the branch of our Government which the most needs support; the other that like the analogous branch in the English Government, it is already too strong for the republican parts of the Constitution. . . . The former of these are called Federalists, sometimes Aristocrats or monocrats & sometimes Tories, after the corresponding Sect in the English Government of exactly the same definition: the latter are still republicans, whigs, Jacobins, Anarchists, disorganizers, etc. These terms are in familiar use with most persons. . . . The most upright and conscientious characters are on both sides [of] the question, and as to myself I can say with truth that political tenets have never taken away my esteem for a moral and good man.

To Abigail Adams, 1804

I tolerate with the utmost latitude the right of others to differ from me in opinion without imputing to them criminality. I know too well the weakness and uncertainty of human reason to wonder at its different results. Both of our political parties, at least the honest part of them, agree conscientiously in the same object—the public good; but they differ essentially in what they deem the means of promoting that good. One side . . . fears most the ignorance of the people; the other, the selfishness of rulers independent of them. Which is right, time and experience will prove. We think that one side of this experiment has been long enough tried, and proved not to promote the good of the many; and that the other has not been fairly and sufficiently tried. Our opponents think the reverse. With whichever opinion the body of the nation concurs, that must prevail. My anxieties on this subject will never carry me beyond the use of fair and honorable means, of truth and reason; nor have they ever lessened my esteem for moral worth, nor alienated my affections from a single friend, who did not first withdraw himself.

Basic differences between the two parties
To Judge Johnson, 1823

The fact is, that at the formation of our government, many had formed their political opinions on European writings and practices, believing the experience of old countries, and especially of England, abusive as it was, to be a safer guide than mere theory. The doctrines of Europe were, that men in numerous associations cannot be restrained within the limits of order and justice, but by forces physical and moral, wielded over them by authorities independent of their will. Hence their organization of kings, hereditary nobles, and priests. Still further to constrain the brute force of the people, they deem it necessary to keep them down by hard labor, poverty and ignorance, and to take from them, as from bees, so much of their earnings, as that unremitting labor shall be necessary to obtain a sufficient surplus barely to sustain a scanty and miserable life. And these earnings they apply to maintain their privileged orders in splendor and idleness, to fascinate the eyes of the people, and excite in them an humble adoration and submission, as to an order of superior beings.

PRINCIPLES OF DEMOCRACY

Although few among us had gone all these lengths of opinion, yet many had advanced, some more, some less, on the way. And in the convention which formed our government, they endeavored to draw the cords of power as tight as they could obtain them, to lessen the dependence of the general functionaries on their constituents, to subject to them those of the States, and to weaken their means of maintaining the steady equilibrium which the majority of the convention had deemed salutary for both branches, general and local. To recover, therefore, in practice the powers which the nation had refused, and to warp to their own wishes those actually given, was the steady object of the federal party.

Ours [the republican party], on the contrary, was to maintain the will of the majority of the convention, and of the people themselves. We believed, with them, that man was a rational animal, endowed by nature with rights and with an innate sense of justice; and that he could be restrained from wrong and protected in right, by moderate powers confided to persons of his own choice, and held to their duties by dependence on his own will. We believed that the complicated organization of kings, nobles, and priests, was not the wisest nor best to effect the happiness of associated man; that wisdom and virtue were not hereditary; that the trappings of such a machinery, consumed by their expense, those earnings of industry, they were meant to protect, and, by the inequalities they produced, exposed liberty to sufferance.

We believed that men, enjoying in ease and security the full fruits of their own industry, enlisted by all their interests on the side of law and order, habituated to think for themselves, and to follow their reason as their guide, would be more easily and safely governed than with minds nourished in error, and vitiated and debased, as in Europe, by ignorance, indigence and oppression. The cherishment of the people then was our principle, the fear and distrust of them, that of the other party. Composed, as we were of the landed and laboring interests of the country, we could not be less anxious for a government of law and order than were the inhabitants of the cities, the strongholds of federalism. And whether our efforts to save the principles and form of our constitution have not been salutary, let the present republican freedom, order and prosperity of our country determine.

CHAPTER III

THE CONSTITUTION

I. DIVISION OF POWERS

To Adams, 1787

THE FIRST principle of a good government, is certainly, a distribution of its powers into executive, judiciary and legislative, and a subdivision of the latter into two or three branches. It is a good step gained, when it is proved that the English constitution, acknowledged to be better than all which have preceded it, is only better in proportion as it has approached nearer to this distribution of powers. From this, the last step is easy, to show by a comparison of our constitutions with that of England, how much more perfect they are.

Notes on Virginia, Query 13

An *elective despotism* was not the government we fought for, but one which should not only be founded on free principles, but in which the powers of the government should be so divided and balanced among several bodies . . . as that no one could transcend their legal limits, without being effectually checked and restrained by the others.

To Madison, 1787

I like the organization of the government into legislative, judiciary and executive. I like the power given the legislature to levy taxes, and for that reason solely, I approve of the greater House being chosen by the people directly. For though I think a House so chosen, will be very far inferior to the present Congress, will be very illy qualified to legislate for the Union, for foreign nations, etc., yet this evil does not weigh against the good, of preserving inviolate the fundamental principle, that the people are not to be taxed but by representatives chosen immediately by themselves.

To Madison, 1787

I am much pleased too, with the substitution of the method of voting by person, instead of that of voting by States; and I like the negative given to the Executive, conjointly with a third of either House; though I should have liked it better, had the judiciary been associated for that purpose, or invested with a similar power. There are other good things of less moment.

II. Bill of Rights

Criticism of the Constitution's shortcomings
To Madison, 1787

I will now tell you what I do not like. First, the omission of a bill of rights, providing clearly, and without the aid of sophism, for freedom of religion, freedom of the press, protection against standing armies, restriction of monopolies, the eternal and unremitting force of the habeas corpus laws, and trials by jury in all matters of fact triable by the laws of the land, and not by the laws of nations.*

The people are entitled to a Bill of Rights
To Madison, 1787

I have a right to nothing, which another has a right to take away; and Congress will have a right to take away trials by jury in all civil cases. Let me add, that a bill of rights is what the people are entitled to against every government on earth, general or particular; and what no just government should refuse, or rest on inference.

To Madison, 1788

But if such cannot be found, then it is better to establish trials by jury, the right of habeas corpus, freedom of the press and freedom of religion, in all cases, and to abolish standing armies in time of peace, and monopolies in all cases, than not to do it in any. The few cases wherein these things may do evil, cannot be weighed against the multitude wherein the want of them will do evil.

Unrestricted right of habeas corpus
To Madison, 1788

Why suspend the habeas corpus in insurrections and rebellions? The parties who may be arrested, may be charged instantly with a well defined crime; of course, the judge will

---

* "Our new constitution is powerfully attacked in the American newspapers. The objections are, that its effect would be to form the thirteen States into one; that, proposing to melt all down into one general government, they have fenced the people by no declaration of rights; they have not renounced the power of keeping a standing army; they have not secured the liberty of the press; they have reserved the power of abolishing trials by jury in civil cases; they have proposed that the laws of the federal legislatures, shall be paramount to the laws and constitutions of the States; they have abandoned rotation in office; and particularly, their President may be re-elected from four years to four years, for life, so as to render him a King for life, like a King of Poland; and they have not given him either the check or aid of a council. To these they add calculations of expense, &c., &c., to frighten the people. You will perceive that these objections are serious, and some of them not without foundation. The constitution, however, has been received with a very general enthusiasm, and as far as can be judged from external demonstrations, the bulk of the people are eager to adopt it." (*To Carmichael, 1787.*)

remand them. If the public safety requires that the government should have a man imprisoned on less probable testimony, in those than in other emergencies, let him be taken and tried, retaken and retried, while the necessity continues, only giving him redress against the government, for damages. Examine the history of England. See how few of the cases of the suspension of the habeas corpus law, have been worthy of that suspension. They have been either real treason, wherein the parties might as well have been charged at once, or sham plots, where it was shameful they should ever have been suspected. Yet for the few cases wherein the suspension of the habeas corpus has done real good, that operation is now become habitual, and the minds of the nation almost prepared to live under its constant suspension.

Suggested amplifications in the Bill of Rights
To Madison, 1789

I must now say a word on the declaration of rights, you have been so good as to send me. I like it, as far as it goes; but I should have been for going further. For instance, the following alterations and additions would have pleased me. Article 4. "The people shall not be deprived of their right to speak, to write, or *otherwise* to publish anything but false facts affecting injuriously the life, liberty, property or reputation of others, or affecting the peace of the confederacy with foreign nations. Article 7. All facts put in issue before any judicature, shall be tried by jury, except, 1, in cases of admiralty jurisdiction, wherein a foreigner shall be interested; 2, in cases cognizable before a court martial, concerning only the regular officers and soldiers of the United States, or members of the militia in actual service in time of war insurrection; and 3, in impeachments allowed by the constitution. Article 8. No person shall be held in confinement more than —— days after he shall have demanded and been refused a writ of habeas corpus by the judge appointed by law, nor more than —— days after such a writ shall have been served on the person holding him in confinement, and no order given on due examination for his remandment or discharge, nor more than —— hours in any place at a greater distance than —— miles from the usual residence of some judge authorized to issue the writ of habeas corpus; nor shall that writ be suspended for any term exceeding one year, nor in any place more than —— miles distant from the State or encampment of enemies or of insurgents. Article 9. Monopolies may be allowed to persons for their own productions in literature, and their own inventions in the arts, for a term not exceeding —— years, but for no longer term, and no other purpose. Article 10. All troops of the United States shall stand *ipso facto* disbanded, at the expiration of the term for which their pay and subsistence shall have been last voted by Congress, and all officers and soldiers, not natives of the United States, shall be incapable of serving in their armies by land, except during a foreign war." These restrictions I think are so guarded, as to hinder evil only.

In the arguments in favor of a declaration of rights, you omit one which has great weight with me; the legal check which it puts in the hands of the judiciary. This is a body, which, if rendered independent and kept strictly to their own department, merits great confidence for their learning and integrity. In fact, what degree of confidence would be too much, for a body composed of such men as Wythe, Blair and Pendleton? On characters like these, the *"civium ardor prava jubentium"* would make no impression. I am happy to find that, on the whole, you are a friend to this amendment. The declaration of rights, is, like all other human blessings, alloyed with some inconveniences, and not accomplishing fully its object. But the good in this instance, vastly overweighs the evil.

I cannot refrain from making short answers to the objections which your letter states to have been raised. 1. That the rights in question are reserved, by the manner in which the federal powers are granted. Answer. A constitutive act may, certainly, be so formed, as to need no declaration of rights. The act itself has the force of a declaration, as far as it goes; and if it goes to all material points, nothing more is wanting. In the draught of a constitution which I had once a thought of proposing in Virginia, and printed afterwards, I endeavored to reach all the great objects of public liberty, and did not mean to add a declaration of rights. Probably the object was imperfectly executed; but the deficiencies would have been supplied by others, in the course of discussion. But in a constitutive act which leaves some precious articles unnoticed, and raises implications against others, a declaration of rights becomes necessary, by way of supplement. This is the case of our new federal Constitution. This instrument forms us into one State, as to certain objects, and gives us a legislative and executive body for these objects. It should, therefore, guard us against their abuses of power, within the field submitted to them.

2. A positive declaration of some essential rights could not be obtained in the requisite latitude. Answer. Half a loaf is better than no bread. If we cannot secure all our rights, let us secure what we can.

3. The limited powers of the federal government, and jealousy of the subordinate governments, afford a security which exists in no other instance. Answer. The first member of this seems resolvable into the first objection before stated. The jealousy of the subordinate governments is a precious reliance. But observe that those governments are only agents. They must have principles furnished them, whereon to found their opposition. The declaration of rights will be the text, whereby they will try all the acts of the federal government. In this view, it is necessary to the federal government also; as by the same text, they may try the opposition of the subordinate governments.

4. Experience proves the inefficacy of a bill of rights. True. But though it is not absolutely efficacious under all circumstances, it is of great potency always, and rarely inefficacious. A brace the more will often keep up the building which would have fallen, with that brace the less. There is a remarkable difference between the characters of the inconveniences which attend a declaration of rights, and those which attend the want of it. The inconveniences of the declaration are, that it may cramp government in its useful exertions. But the evil of this is short-lived, moderate and reparable. The inconveniences of the want of a declaration are permanent, afflicting and irreparable. They are in constant progression from bad to worse.

The executive, in our governments, is not the sole, it is scarcely the principal object of my jealousy. The tyranny of the legislatures is the most formidable dread at present, and will be for many years. That of the executive will come in its turn; but it will be at a remote period. I know there are some among us, who would now establish a monarchy. But they are inconsiderable in number and weight of character. The rising race are all republicans. We were educated in royalism; no wonder, if some of us retain that idolatry still. Our young people are educated in republicanism; an apostasy from that to royalism, is unprecedented and impossible.

How to ameliorate the Constitution
To Madison, 1787

I do not pretend to decide, what would be the best method of procuring the establishment of the manifold good things in this constitution, and of getting rid of the bad. Whether by adopting it, in hopes of future amendment; or after it shall have been duly weighed and canvassed by the people, after seeing the parts they generally dislike, and those they generally approve, to say to them, "We see now what you wish. You are willing to give to your federal government such and such powers; but you wish, at the same time, to have such and such fundamental rights secured to you, and certain sources of convulsion taken away. Be it so. Send together deputies again. Let them establish your fundamental rights by a sacrosanct declaration, and let them pass the parts of the constitution you have approved. These will give powers to your federal government sufficient for your happiness."

This is what might be said, and would probably produce a speedy, more perfect and more permanent form of government. At all events, I hope you will not be discouraged from making other trials, if the present one should fail. We are never permitted to despair of the commonwealth.

To Stuart, 1791

I would rather be exposed to the inconveniences attending too much liberty, than those attending too small a degree of it. Then it is important to strengthen the State governments; and as this cannot be done by any change in the federal constitution, (for the preservation of that is all we need contend for), it must be done by the States themselves, erecting such barriers at the constitutional line as cannot be surmounted either by themselves or by the general government. The only barrier in their power is a wise government. A weak one will lose ground in every contest. To obtain a wise and an able government, I consider the following changes as important. Render the legislature a desirable station by lessening the number of representatives (say to 100) and lengthening somewhat their term, and proportion them equally among the electors. Adopt also a better mode of appointing senators. Render the Executive a more desirable post to men of abilities by making it more independent of the legislature. To wit, let him be chosen by other electors, for a longer time, and ineligible forever after. Responsibility is a tremendous engine in a free government. Let him feel the whole weight of it then, by taking away the shelter of his executive council. Experience both ways has already established the superiority of this measure. Render the judiciary respectable by every possible means, to wit, firm tenure in office, competent salaries, and reduction of their numbers. Men of high learning and abilities are few in every country; and by taking in those who are not so, the able part of the body have their hands tied by the unable. This branch of the government will have the weight of the conflict on their hands, because they will be the last appeal of reason. These are my general ideas of amendments; but, preserving the ends, I should be flexible and conciliatory as to the means.

III. States' Rights

A beautiful equilibrium
To P. Fitzhugh, 1798

I do not think it for the interest of the general government itself, and still less of the Union at large, that the State governments should be so little respected as they have been. However, I dare say that in time all these as well as their central government, like the planets revolving round their common sun, acting and acted upon according to their respective weights and distances, will produce that beautiful equilibrium on which our Constitution is founded, and which I believe it will exhibit to the world in a degree of perfection, unexampled but in the planetary system itself. The enlightened statesman, therefore, will endeavor to preserve the weight and influence of every part, as too much given to any member of it would destroy the general equilibrium.

State governments are barriers of our liberty
To De Tracy, 1811

But the true barriers of our liberty in this country are our State governments; and the wisest conservative power ever contrived by man, is that which our Revolution and present government found us possessed. Seventeen distinct States, amalgamated into one as to their foreign concerns, but single and independent as to their internal administration, regularly organized with a legislature and governor resting on the choice of the people, and enlightened by a free press, can never be so fascinated by the arts of one man, as to submit voluntarily to his usurpation. Nor can they be constrained to it by any force he can possess. While that may paralyze the single State in which it happens to be encamped, sixteen others, spread over a country of two thousand miles diameter, rise up on every side, ready organized for deliberation by a constitutional legislature, and for action by their governor, constitutionally the commander of the militia of the State, that is to say, of every man in it able to bear arms; and that militia, too, regularly formed into regiments and battalions, into infantry, cavalry and artillery. . . .

The republican government of France was lost without a struggle, because the party of *"un et indivisible"* had prevailed; no provincial organizations existed to which the people might rally under authority of the laws, the seats of the directory were virtually vacant, and a small force sufficed to turn the legislature out of their chamber, and to salute its leader chief of the nation. But with us, sixteen out of seventeen States rising in mass, under regular organization, and legal commanders, united in object and action by their Congress or, if that be in *duresse,* by a special convention, present such obstacles to an usurper as forever to stifle ambition in the first conception of that object.

State and Federal governments are equal partners
To—(?), 1821

It is a fatal heresy to suppose that either our State governments are superior to the federal, or the federal to the States. The people, to whom all authority belongs, have divided the powers of government into two distinct departments, the leading characters of which are *foreign* and domestic; and they have appointed for each a distinct set of functionaries. These they have made coordinate, checking and balancing each other, like the three cardinal departments in the individual States; each equally supreme as to the powers delegated to itself, and neither authorized ultimately to decide what belongs to itself, or to its coparcener in government. As independent, in fact, as different nations, a spirit of forbearance and compromise, therefore, and not of encroachment and usurpation, is the healing balm of such a constitution; and each party should prudently shrink from all approach to the line of demarcation, instead of rashly overleaping it, or throwing grapples ahead to haul to hereafter. But finally, the peculiar happiness of our blessed system is, that in differences of opinion between these different sets of servants, the appeal is to neither, but to their employers peaceably assembled by their representatives in Convention. This is more rational than the *jus fortioris,* or the cannon's mouth, the *ultima et sola ratio regum.*

States should oppose Federal usurpation
To W. B. Giles, 1825

I see. . . with the deepest affliction, the rapid strides with which the federal branch of our government is advancing towards the usurpation of all the rights reserved to the States, and the consolidation in itself of all powers, foreign and domestic; and that too, by constructions which, if legitimate, leave no limits to their power. . . . It is but too evident that the three ruling branches [of the federal government] are in combination to strip their colleagues, the State authorities, of the powers reserved by them. . . .

Under the power to regulate commerce, they assume indefinitely that also over agriculture and manufactures, and call it regulation to take the earnings of one of these branches of industry, and that too the most depressed, and put them into the pockets of the other, the most flourishing of all. Under the authority to establish post roads, they claim that of cutting down mountains for the construction of roads, of digging canals, and aided by a little sophistry on the words "general welfare," a right to do, not only the acts to effect that, which are specifically enumerated and permitted, but whatsoever they shall think, or pretend will be for the general welfare.

And what is our resource for the preservation of the constitution? Reason and argument? You might as well reason and argue with the marble columns encircling them. The representatives chosen by ourselves? They are joined in the combination, some from incorrect views of government, some from corrupt ones, sufficient voting together to out-number the sound parts; and with majorities only of one, two, or three, bold enough to go forward in defiance.

Are we then *to stand to our arms* . . . ? No. That must be the last resource, not to be thought of until much longer and greater sufferings. If every infraction of a compact of so many parties is to be resisted at once, as a dissolution of it, none can ever be formed which would last one year. We must have patience and longer endurance then with our brethren while under delusion; give them time for reflection and experience of consequences; keep ourselves in a situation to profit by the chapter of accidents; and separate from our companions only when the sole alternatives left, are the dissolution of our Union with them, or submission to a government without limitation of powers. Between these two evils, when we must make a choice, there can be no hesitation.

But in the meanwhile, the States should be watchful to note every material usurpation on their rights; to denounce them as they occur in the most peremptory terms; to protest against them as wrongs to which our present submission shall be considered, not as acknowledgments or precedents of rights, but as a temporary yielding to the lesser evil, until their accumulation shall overweigh that of separation. I would go still further, and give to the federal member, by a regular amendment of the constitution, a right to make roads and canals of intercommunication between the States, providing sufficiently against corrupt practices in Congress [log-rolling, etc.] by declaring that the federal proportion of each State of the moneys so employed, shall be in works within the State, or elsewhere with its consent, and with a due *salvo* of jurisdiction. This is the course which I think safest and best as yet.

IV. THE PRESIDENCY

To avoid despotism
Notes on Virginia, Query 13

Human nature is the same on every side of the Atlantic, and will be alike influenced by the same causes. The time to guard against corruption and tyranny, is before they shall have gotten hold of us. It is better to keep the wolf out of the fold, than to trust to drawing his teeth and claws after he shall have entered.

Danger of Presidential despotism
To Madison, 1787

The second feature I dislike, and strongly dislike, is the abandonment, in every instance, of the principle of rotation in office, and most particularly in the case of the President. Reason and experience tell us, that the first magistrate will always be reëlected if he may be reëlected. He is then an officer for life. This once observed, it becomes of so much consequence to certain nations, to have a friend or a foe at the head of our affairs, that they will interfere with money and with arms. A Galloman, or an Angloman, will be supported by the nation he befriends. If once elected, and at a second or third election outvoted by one or two votes, he will pretend false votes, foul play, hold possession of the reins of government, be supported by the States voting for him, especially if they be the central ones, lying in a compact body themselves, and separating their opponents; and they will be aided by one nation in Europe, while the majority are aided by another. The election of a President of America, some years hence, will be much more interesting to certain nations of Europe, than ever the election of a King of Poland was. Reflect on all the instances in history, ancient and modern, of elective monarchies, and say if they do not give foundations for my fears; the Roman Emperors, the Popes while they were of any importance, the German Emperors till they became hereditary in practice, the Kings of Poland, the Deys of the Ottoman dependencies. It may be said, that if elections are to be attended with these disorders, the less frequently they are repeated the better. But experience says, that to free them from disorder, they must be rendered less interesting by a necessity of change. No foreign power, nor domestic party, will waste their blood and money to elect a person, who must go out at the end of a short period.

To Adams, 1787

How do you like our new constitution? . . . Their President seems a bad edition of a Polish King. He may be elected from four years to four years, for life. Reason and experience prove to us, that a chief magistrate, so continuable, is an office for life. When one or two generations shall have proved that this is an office for life, it becomes, on every occasion, worthy of intrigue, of bribery, of force, and even of foreign interference. It will be of great consequence to France and England, to have America governed by a Galloman or Angloman. Once in office, and possessing the military force of the Union, without the aid or check of a council, he would not be easily dethroned, even if the people could be induced to withdraw their votes from him. I wish that at the end of the four years, they had made him forever ineligible a second time.

Fears perpetual re-eligibility of the President
To Washington, 1788

There are two things, however, which I dislike strongly. 1. The want of a declaration of rights. I am in hopes the opposition of Virginia will remedy this, and produce such a declaration. 2. The perpetual re-eligibility of the President. This, I fear, will make that an office for life, first, and then hereditary. I was much an enemy to monarchies before I came to Europe. I am ten thousand times more so, since I have seen what they are. There is scarcely an evil known in these countries, which may not be traced to their king, as its source, nor a good, which is not derived from the small fibers of republicanism existing among them. I can further say, with safety, there is not a crowned head in Europe, whose talents or merits would entitle him to be elected a vestryman, by the people of any parish in America.

To Carrington, 1788

Re-eligibility makes him [the President] an officer for life, and the disasters inseparable from an elective monarchy, render it preferable if we cannot tread back that step, that we should go forward and take refuge in an hereditary one. Of the correction of this article [Amendment], however, I entertain no present hope, because I find it has scarcely excited an objection in America. And if it does not take place ere long, it assuredly never will. The natural progress of things is for liberty to yield and government to gain ground. As yet our spirits are free. Our jealousy is only put to sleep by the unlimited confidence we all repose in the person to whom we all look as our president.* After him inferior characters may perhaps succeed, and awaken us to the danger which his merit has led us into.

Urges Washington to run again
To Washington, 1792

The confidence of the whole Union is centered in you. Your being at the helm will be more than an answer to every argument which can be used to alarm and lead the people in any quarter, into violence and secession. North and South will hang together if they have you to hang on; and if the first correction of a numerous representation should fail in its effect, your presence will give time for trying others, not inconsistent with the union and peace of the States.

* George Washington.

I am perfectly aware of the oppression under which your present office lays your mind, and of the ardor with which you pant for domestic life.* But there is sometimes an eminence of character on which society have such peculiar claims as to control the predilections of the individual for a particular walk of happiness, and restrain him to that alone arising from the present and future benedictions of mankind. This seems to be your condition, and the law imposed on you by providence in forming your character, and fashioning the events on which it was to operate; and it is to motives like these, and not to personal anxieties of mine or others who have no right to call on you for sacrifices, that I appeal, and urge a revisal of it, on the ground of change in the aspect of things.

President Washington's political beliefs
To J. Melish, 1813

General Washington did not harbor one principle of federalism. He was neither an Angloman, a monarchist, nor a separatist. He sincerely wished the people to have as much self-government as they were competent to exercise themselves. The only point on which he and I ever differed in opinion, was, that I had more confidence than he had in the natural integrity and discretion of the people, and in the safety and extent to which they might trust themselves with a control over their government. He has asseverated to me a thousand times his determination that the existing government should have a fair trial, and that in support of it he would spend the last drop of his blood.

Two four-year terms for the Presidency
To John Taylor, 1805

I have since become sensible that 7 years is too long to be irrevocable, and that there should be a peaceable way of withdrawing a man in midway who is wrong-doing. The service

* "The President is not well. Little lingering fevers have been hanging about him for a week or ten days, and affected his looks most remarkably. He is also extremely affected by the attacks made and kept up on him in the public papers. I think he feels those things more than any person I ever yet met with. I am sincerely sorry to see them. I remember an observation of yours, made when I first went to New York, that the satellites and sycophants which surrounded him had wound up the ceremonials of the government to a pitch of stateliness which nothing but his personal character could have supported, and which no character after him could ever maintain. It appears now that even his will be insufficient to justify them in the appeal of the times to common sense as the arbiter of everything. Naked he would have been sanctimoniously reverenced; but enveloped in the rays of royalty, they can hardly be torn off without laceration. It is the more unfortunate that his attack is planted on popular ground, on the love of the people to France and its cause, which is universal." *(To Madison, 1793.)*

for 8 years with a power to remove at the end of the first four, comes nearly to my principle as corrected by experience. And it is in adherence to that that I determined to withdraw at the end of my second term. The danger is that the indulgence and attachments of the people will keep a man in the chair after he becomes a dotard, that reëlection through life shall become habitual, and election for life follow that. General Washington set the example of voluntary retirement after 8 years. I shall follow it, and a few more precedents will oppose the obstacle of habit to any one after a while who shall endeavor to extend his term.

Advantages of a single over a plural executive
To De Tracy, 1811

When our present government was established, we had ... many leanings towards a supreme executive counsel. It happened that at that time the experiment of such an one was commenced in France, while the single executive was under trial here. We watched the motions and effects of these two rival plans, with an interest and anxiety proportioned to the importance of a choice between them. The experiment in France failed after a short course ... from those internal jealousies and dissensions in the Directory, which will ever arise among men equal in power, without a principal to decide and control their differences. We had tried a similar experiment in 1784, by establishing a committee of the States, composed of a member from every State, then thirteen, to exercise the executive functions during the recess of Congress. They fell immediately into schisms and dissensions, which became at length so inveterate as to render all coöperation among them impracticable; they dissolved themselves, abandoning the helm of government, and it continued without a head, until Congress met the ensuing winter. This was then imputed to the temper of two or three individuals; but the wise ascribed it to the nature of man.

The failure of the French Directory, and from the same cause, seems to have authorized a belief that the form of a plurality, however promising in theory, is impracticable with men constituted with the ordinary passions. While the tranquil and steady tenor of our single executive, during a course of twenty-two years of the most tempestuous times the history of the world has ever presented, gives a rational hope that this important problem is at length solved.

Aided by the counsels of a cabinet . . . , the President . . . has the benefit of their wisdom and information, brings their views to one center, and produces an unity of action and direction in all the branches of the government.

The excellence of this construction of the executive power has already manifested itself here. . . . During the administration of our first President, his cabinet of four members was equally divided by as marked an opposition of principle as monarchism and republicanism could bring into conflict. Had that cabinet been a directory, like positive and negative quantities in algebra, the opposing wills would have balanced each other and produced a state of absolute inaction. But the President heard with calmness the opinions and reasons of each, decided the course to be pursued, and kept the government steadily in it, unaffected by the agitation. The public knew well the dissensions of the cabinet, but never had an uneasy thought on their account, because they knew also they had provided a regulating power which would keep the machine in steady movement. I speak with an intimate knowledge of these scenes, *quorum pars fui.* . . .*

The third administration† which was of eight years, presented an example of harmony in a cabinet of six persons, to which perhaps history has furnished no parallel. There never arose, during the whole time, an instance of an unpleasant thought or word between the members. We sometimes met under differences of opinion, but scarcely ever failed, by conversing and reasoning, so to modify each other's ideas, as to produce an unanimous result. Yet, able and amicable as these members were, I am not certain this would have been the case, had each possessed equal and independent powers. Ill-defined limits of their respective departments, jealousies, trifling at first, but nourished and strengthened by repetition of occasions, intrigues without doors of designing persons to build an importance to themselves on the divisions of others, might, from small beginnings, have produced persevering oppositions. But the power of decision in the President left no object for internal dissension, and external intrigue was stifled in embryo by the knowledge which incendiaries possessed, that no division they could foment would change the course of the executive power.

I am not conscious that my participations in executive authority have produced any bias in favor of the single exec-

* "Of which I was a part."
†Jefferson's own: 1801-09.

utive; because the parts I have acted have been in the subordinate, as well as superior stations, and because, if I know myself, what I have felt, and what I have wished, I know that I have never been so well pleased, as when I could shift power from my own, on the shoulders of others; nor have I ever been able to conceive how any rational being could propose happiness to himself from the exercise of power over others. . . .

A single executive, with eminence of talent and destitution of principle, equal to the object, might, by usurpation, render his powers hereditary. Yet I think history furnishes as many examples of a single usurper arising out of a government by a plurality, as of temporary trusts of power in a single hand rendered permanent by usurpation. I do not believe, therefore, that this danger is lessened in the hands of a plural executive. Perhaps it is greatly increased, by the state of inefficiency to which they are liable from feuds and divisions among themselves.

V. JUDICIARY

Necessity for an upright and independent judiciary
To G. Wythe, 1776

The dignity and stability of government in all its branches, the morals of the people, and every blessing of society, depend so much upon an upright and skilful administration of justice, that the judicial power ought to be distinct from both the legislative and executive, and independent upon both, that so it may be a check upon both, as both should be checks upon that. The judges, therefore, should always be men of learning and experience in the laws, of exemplary morals, great patience, calmness and attention; their minds should not be distracted with jarring interests; they should not be dependent upon any man or body of men. To these ends they should hold estates for life in their offices, or, in other words, their commissions should be during good behavior, and their salaries ascertained and established by law.

For misbehavior, the grand inquest of the colony, the house of representatives, should impeach them before the governor and council, when they should have time and opportunity to make their defense; but if convicted, should be removed from their offices, and subjected to such other punishment as shall be thought proper.

The people should exercise control over the judges
To Arnoud, 1789

We think, in America, that it is necessary to introduce the people into every department of government, as far as they are capable of exercising it; and that this is the only way to insure a long-continued and honest administration of its powers.

1. They are not qualified to exercise themselves the executive department, but they are qualified to name the person who shall exercise it. With us, therefore, they choose this officer every four years. 2. They are not qualified to legislate. With us, therefore, they only choose the legislators. 3. They are not qualified to *judge* questions of *law,* but they are very capable of judging questions of *fact*. In the form of juries, therefore, they determine all matters of fact, leaving to the permanent judges, to decide the law resulting from those facts. But we all know that permanent judges acquire an *Esprit de corps;* that being known, they are liable to be tempted by bribery; that they are misled by favor, by relationship, by a spirit of party, by a devotion to the executive or legislative power; that it is better to leave a cause to the decision of cross and pile, than to that of a judge biased to one side; and that the opinion of twelve honest jurymen gives still a better hope of right, than cross and pile does. It is in the power, therefore, of the juries, if they think permanent judges are under any bias whatever, in any cause, to take on themselves to judge the law as well as the fact. They never exercise this power but when they suspect partiality in the judges; and by the exercise of this power, they have been the firmest bulwarks of English liberty. Were I called upon to decide, whether the people had best be omitted in the legislative or judiciary department, I would say it is better to leave them out of the legislative. The execution of the laws is more important than the making of them. However, it is best to have the people in all the three departments, where that is possible.

Judges should be elected by the people
To S. Kercheval, 1816

It has been thought that the people are not competent electors of judges *learned in the law*. But I do not know that this is true, and, if doubtful, we should follow principle. In this, as in many other elections, they would be guided by reputation, which would not err oftener, perhaps, than the present mode of appointment. In one State of the Union, at least, it has long been tried, and with the most satisfactory success. The judges of Connecticut have been chosen by the people every six months, for nearly two centuries, and I believe there has hardly ever been an instance of change; so powerful is the curb of incessant responsibility.

If prejudice, however, derived from a monarchical institution, is still to prevail against the vital elective principle of our own, and if the existing example among ourselves of periodical election of judges by the people be still mistrusted, let us at least not adopt the evil, and reject the good, of the English precedent; let us retain amovability on the concurrence of the executive and legislative branches, and nomination by the executive alone. Nomination to office is an executive function. To give it to the legislature, as we do, is a violation of the principle of the separation of powers. It swerves the members from correctness, by temptations to intrigue for office themselves, and to a corrupt barter of votes; and destroys responsibility by dividing it among a multitude. By leaving nomination in its proper place, among executive functions, the principle of the distribution of power is preserved, and responsibility weighs with its heaviest force on a single head.

Judicial usurpation in constitutional matters
To T. Ritchie, 1820

The judiciary of the United States is the subtle corps of sappers and miners constantly working under ground to undermine the foundations of our confederated fabric. They are construing our constitution from a coordination of a general and special government to a general and supreme one alone. This will lay all things at their feet. . . . We shall see if they are bold enough to take the daring stride their five lawyers have lately taken. If they do, then . . . I will say, that "against this every man should raise his voice," and more, should uplift his arm. . . .

Having found, from experience that impeachment is an impracticable thing, a mere scare-crow, they consider themselves secure for life; they sculk from responsibility to public opinion. . . . An opinion is huddled up in conclave, perhaps by a majority of one, delivered as if unanimous, and with the silent acquiescence of lazy or timid associates, by a crafty chief judge, who sophisticates the law to his mind, by the turn of his own reasoning. . . .

A judiciary independent of a king or executive alone, is a good thing; but independence of the will of the nation is a solecism, at least in a republican government.

A usurping judiciary will become a despotism
To Jarvis, 1820

To consider the judges as the ultimate arbiters of all constitutional questions [is] a very dangerous doctrine indeed, and one which would place us under the despotism of an oligarchy. Our judges are as honest as other men, and not more so. They have, with others, the same passions for party, for power, and the privilege of their corps. Their maxim is *"boni judicis est ampliare jurisdictionem,"* and their power the more dangerous as they are in office for life. . . . The constitution has erected no such single tribunal, knowing that to whatever hands confided, with the corruptions of time and party, its members would become despots.

If the Federal judiciary is not checked, it will destroy democracy.
To C. Hammond, 1821

It has long, however, been my opinion, and I have never shrunk from its expression (although I do not choose to put it into a newspaper, nor, like a Priam in armor, offer myself its champion), that the germ of dissolution of our federal government is in the constitution of the federal judiciary; an irresponsible body (for impeachment is scarcely a scare-crow) working like gravity by night and by day, gaining a little to-day and little to-morrow, and advancing its noiseless step like a thief, over the field of jurisdiction, until all shall be usurped from the States, and the government of all be consolidated into one. To this I am opposed; because, when all government, domestic and foreign, in little as in great things, shall be drawn to Washington as the center of all power, it will render powerless the checks provided of one government or another, and will become as venal and oppressive as the government from which we separated. It will be as in Europe, where every man must be either pike or gudgeon, hammer or anvil. Our functionaries and theirs are wares from the same work-shop; made of the same materials, and by the same hand. If the States look with apathy on this silent descent of their government into the gulf which is to swallow all, we have only to weep over the human character formed uncontrollable but by a rod of iron, and the blasphemers of man, as incapable of self-government, become his true historians.

Sinister procedure of the Supreme Court
To Pleasants, 1821

Another most condemnable practice of the Supreme Court to be corrected is that of cooking up a decision in caucus and delivering it by one of their members as the opinion of the court, without the possibility of our knowing how many, who, and for what reasons each member concurred. This completely defeats the possibility of impeachment by smothering evidence. A regard for character in each being now the only hold we can have of them, we should hold fast to it. They would, were they to give their opinions seriatim and publicly, endeavor to justify themselves to the world by explaining the reasons which led to their opinion.

To curb Federal judges, they should be appointed every six years
To Pleasants, 1821

[For the] difficult task in curbing the Judiciary in their enterprises on the Constitution . . . the best [remedy] I can devise would be to give future commissions to judges for six years [the Senatorial term] with a re-appointmentability by the president with the approbation of *both* houses. If this would not be independence enough, I know not what would be. . . .

The Judiciary perversions of the Constitution will forever be protected under the pretext of errors of judgment, which by principle are exempt from punishment. Impeachment therefore is a bugbear which they fear not at all. But they would be under some awe of the canvas of their conduct which would be open to both houses regularly every sixth year. It is a misnomer to call a government republican, in which a branch of the supreme power is independent of the nation.

To W. T. Barry, 1822

If ever this vast country is brought under a single government, it will be one of the most extensive corruption, indifferent and incapable of a wholesome care over so wide a spread of surface. This will not be borne, and you will have to choose between reformation and revolution. If I know the spirit of this country, the one or the other is inevitable. Before the canker is become inveterate, before its venom has reached so much of the body politic as to get beyond control, remedy should be applied. Let the future appointments of judges be for four or six years, and renewable by the President and Senate. This will bring their conduct, at regular periods, under revision and probation, and may keep them in equipose between the general and special governments. We have erred in this point, by copying England, where certainly it is a good thing to have the judges independent of the King. But we have omitted to copy their caution also, which makes a judge removable on the address of both legislative Houses. That there should be public functionaries independent of the nation, whatever may be their demerit, is a solecism in a republic, of the first order of absurdity and inconsistency.

VI. Subject to Change

The Constitution—wisest ever made
To Humphreys, 1789

The operations which have taken place in America lately, fill me with pleasure. In the first place, they realize the confidence I had, that whenever our affairs go obviously wrong, the good sense of the people will interpose, and set them to rights. The example of changing a constitution, by assembling the wise men of the State, instead of assembling armies, will be worth as much to the world as the former examples we had given them. The Constitution, too, which was the result of our deliberations, is unquestionably the wisest ever yet presented to men.

To A. Marsh, 1801: N. Y. Pub. Lib., MS, II, 84

The Constitution of the United States [is] the result of the collected wisdom of our country. That wisdom has committed to us the important task of proving by example that a government if organized in all its parts on the Representative principle unadulterated by the infusion of spurious elements, if founded, not in the fears and follies of man, but on his reason, on his sense of right, on the predominance of the social over his dissocial passions, may be so free as to restrain him in no moral right, and so firm as to protect him from every moral wrong.

THE CONSTITUTION

A written Constitution fixes political principles
To Dr. Priestley, 1802

I was in Europe when the Constitution was planned, and never saw it till after it was established. On receiving it I wrote strongly to Mr. Madison, urging the want of provision for the freedom of religion, freedom of the press, trial by jury, habeas corpus, the substitution of militia for a standing army, and an express reservation to the States of all rights not specifically granted to the Union. He accordingly moved in the first session of Congress for these amendments, which were agreed to and ratified by the States as they now stand. This is all the hand I had in what related to the Constitution. . . . It is certain that though written constitutions may be violated in moments of passion or delusion, yet they furnish a text to which those who are watchful may again rally and recall the people; they fix too for the people the principles of their political creed.

But constitutions are not sacred
To S. Kercheval, 1816

Some men look at constitutions with sanctimonious reverence and deem them like the ark of the covenant, too sacred to be touched. They ascribe to the men of the preceding age a wisdom more than human, and suppose what they did to be beyond amendment. . . . I am certainly not an advocate for frequent and untried changes in laws and constitutions. I think moderate imperfections had better be borne with. . . . But I know also that laws and institutions must go hand in hand with the progress of the human mind. . . . As new discoveries are made, new truths disclosed, and manners and opinions change with the change of circumstances, institutions must advance also, and keep pace with the times. We might as well require a man to wear still the coat which fitted him when a boy, as civilized society to remain ever under the regimen of their barbarous ancestors. . . . Each generation . . . has a right to choose for itself the form of government it believes the most promotive of its own happiness. . . . A solemn opportunity of doing this every 19 or 20 years should be provided by the constitution. . . . This corporeal globe, and everything upon it, belong to its present corporeal inhabitants, during their generation. They alone have a right to direct what is the concern of themselves alone. . . . If this avenue be shut . . . , it will make itself heard through that of force, and we shall go on, as other nations are doing, in the endless circle of oppressions, rebellions, reformations; and oppression, rebellion, reformation, again; and so on forever.

—*Nor permanent*
To J. Cartwright, 1824

Can they [our constitutional laws] be made unchangeable? Can one generation bind another, and all others, in succession forever? I think not. The Creator has made the earth for the living, not the dead. Rights and powers can only belong to persons, not to things, not to mere matter, unendowed with will. The dead are not even things. . . . To what then are attached the rights and powers they held while in the form of men? A generation may bind itself as long as its majority is in place, holds all the rights and powers their predecessors once held, and may change their laws and institutions to suit themselves. Nothing then is unchangeable but the inherent and unalienable rights of man.

CHAPTER IV

POLITICAL ECONOMY

I. AGRICULTURE AND COMMERCE

Advantages of an agricultural over a commercial economy
To Jay, 1785

WE HAVE now lands enough to employ an infinite number of people in their cultivation. Cultivators of the earth are the most valuable citizens. They are the most vigorous, the most independent, the most virtuous, and they are tied to their country, and wedded to its liberty and interests, by the most lasting bonds. As long, therefore, as they can find employment in this line, I would not convert them into mariners, artisans, or anything else. But our citizens will find employment in this line, till their numbers, and of course their productions, become too great for the demand, both internal and foreign. This is not the case as yet, and probably will not be for a considerable time. As soon as it is, the surplus of hands must be turned to something else. I should then, perhaps, wish to turn them to the sea in preference to manufactures; because, comparing the characters of the two classes, I find the former the most valuable citizens. I consider the class of artificers as the panders of vice, and the instruments by which the liberties of a country are generally overturned. . . . Our people are decided in the opinion, that it is necessary for us to take a share in the occupation of the ocean, and their established habits induce them to require that the sea be kept open to them.

But what will be the consequence? Frequent wars without a doubt. Their property will be violated on the sea, and in foreign ports, their persons will be insulted, imprisoned, &c., for pretended debts, contracts, crimes, contraband, &c., &c. These insults must be resented, even if we had no feelings, yet to prevent their eternal repetition; or, in other words, our commerce on the ocean and in other countries, must be paid for by frequent war. The justest dispositions possible in ourselves, will not secure us against it. It would be necessary that all other nations were just also. Justice indeed, on our part, will save us from those wars which would have been produced by a contrary disposition. But how can we prevent those produced by the wrongs of other nations? By putting ourselves in a condition to punish them. . . . *because an insult unpunished is the parent of many others.*

To Hogendorp, 1785

You ask what I think on the expediency of encouraging our States to be commercial? Were I to indulge my own theory, I should wish them to practise neither commerce nor navigation, but to stand, with respect to Europe, precisely on the footing of China. We should thus avoid wars, and all our citizens would be husbandmen. Whenever, indeed, our numbers should so increase so that our produce would overstock the markets of those nations who should come to seek it, the farmers must employ the surplus of their time in manufactures, or the surplus of our hands must be employed in manufactures or in navigation. But that day would, I think, be distant, and we should long keep our workmen in Europe, while Europe should be drawing rough materials, and even subsistence from America.

Agriculturalists are God's chosen people
Notes on Virginia, Query 19

Those who labor in the earth are the chosen people of God, if ever He had a chosen people, whose breasts He has made His peculiar deposit for substantial and genuine virtue. It is the focus in which he keeps alive that sacred fire, which otherwise might escape from the face of the earth. Corruption of morals in the mass of cultivators is a phenomenon of which no age nor nation has furnished an example. It is the mark set on those, who, not looking up to heaven, to their own soil and industry, as does the husbandman, for their subsistence, depend for it on casualties and caprice of customers. Dependence begets subservience and venality, suffocates the germ of virtue, and prepares fit tools for the designs of ambition. . . .

Generally speaking, the proportion which the aggregate of the other classes of citizens bears in any State to that of its husbandmen, is the proportion of its unsound to its healthy parts, and is a good enough barometer whereby to measure its degree of corruption. While we have land to labor then, let us never wish to see our citizens occupied at a work-bench, or twirling a distaff. Carpenters, masons, smiths, are wanting in husbandry; but, for the general operations of manufacture, let our workshops remain in Europe. It is better to carry provisions and materials to workmen there, than bring them to the provisions and materials, and with them their manners and principles. The loss by the transportation of commodities across the Atlantic will be made up in happiness and permanence of government. The mobs of great cities add just so much to the support of pure government, as sores do to the strength of the human body.

Urbanization would destroy democracy
To Madison, 1787

This reliance cannot deceive us, as long as we remain virtuous; and I think we shall be so, as long as agriculture is our principal object, which will be the case, while there remain vacant lands in any part of America. When we get piled upon one another in large cities, as in Europe, we shall become corrupt as in Europe, and go to eating one another as they do there.

Should America devote herself exclusively to agriculture?
To Say, 1804

The differences of circumstance between this and the old countries of Europe, furnish differences of fact whereon to reason in questions of political economy. . . . There, for instance, the quantity of food is fixed, or increasing in a slow and only arithmetical ratio. . . . Here the immense extent of uncultivated and fertile lands enables every one who will labor to marry young, and to raise a family of any size. Our food, then, may increase geometrically with our laborers, and our births, however multiplied, become effective.

Again, there the best distribution of labor is supposed to be that which places the manufacturing hands alongside the agricultural; so that the one part shall feed both, and the other part furnish both with clothes and other comforts. Would that be best here? Egoism and first appearances say yes. Or would it be better that all our laborers should be employed in agriculture? In this case a double or treble portion of fertile lands would be brought into culture; a double or treble creation of food be produced, and its surplus go to nourish the now perishing births of Europe, who in return would manufacture and send us in exchange our clothes and other comforts. Morality listens to this, and so invariably do the laws of nature create our duties and interests. . . . In solving this question, too, we should allow its just weight to the moral and physical preference of the agricultural, over the manufacturing, man. My occupations permit me only to ask questions. They deny me the time, if I had the information, to answer them.

II. PUBLIC DEBT

One generation has no right to incur debts for another
To Madison, 1789

The question, whether one generation of men has a right to bind another, seems never to have been started either on this or our side of the water. Yet it is a question of such consequences as not only to merit decision, but place also among the fundamental principles of every government. The course of reflection in which we are immersed here, on the elementary principles of society, has presented this question to my mind; and that no such obligation can be transmitted, I think very capable of proof. I set out on this ground, which I suppose to be self-evident, that the *earth belongs in usufruct to the living;* that the dead have neither powers nor rights over it. The portion occupied by any individual ceases to be his when himself ceases to be, and reverts to the society. If the society has formed no rules for the appropriation of its lands in severalty, it will be taken by the first occupants, and these will generally be the wife and children of the decedent. If they have formed rules of appropriation, those rules may give it to the wife and children, or to some one of them, or to the legatee of the deceased. So they may give it to its creditor. But the child, the legatee or creditor, takes it, not by natural right, but by a law of the society of which he is a member, and to which he is subject. Then, no man can, by *natural right*, oblige the lands he occupied, or the persons who succeed him in that occupation, to the payment of debts contracted by him. For if he could, he might during his own life, eat up the usufruct of the lands for several generations to come; and then the lands would belong to the dead, and not to the living, which is the reverse of our principle.

What is true of every member of the society, individually, is true of them all collectively; since the rights of the whole can be no more than the sum of the rights of the individuals. To keep our ideas clear when applying them to a multitude, let us suppose a whole generation of men to be born on the same day, to attain mature age on the same day, and to die on the same day, leaving a succeeding generation in the moment of attaining their mature age, all together. Let the ripe age be supposed of twenty-one years, and their period of life thirty-four years more, that being the average term given by the bills of mortality to persons of twenty-one years of age. Each successive generation would, in this way, come and go off the stage at a fixed moment, as individuals do now. Then I say, the earth belongs to each of these generations during its course, fully and in its own right. The second generation receives it clear of the debts and incumbrances of the first, the third of the second, and so on. For if the first could charge it with a debt, then the earth would belong to the dead and not to the living generation. Then, no generation can contract debts greater than may be paid during the course of its own existence. At twenty-one years of age, they may bind themselves and their lands for thirty-four years to come; at twenty-two, for thirty-three; at twenty-three, for thirty-two; and at fifty-four, for one year only; because these are the terms of life which remain to them at the respective epochs. But a material difference must be noted, between the succession of an individual and that of a whole generation. Individuals are parts only of a society, subject to the laws of a whole. These laws may appropriate the portion of land occupied by a decendent, to his creditor, rather than to any other, or to his child, on condition he satisfies the creditor. But when a whole generation, that is, the whole society, dies, as in the case we have supposed, and another generation or society succeeds, this forms a whole, and there is no superior who can give their territory to a third society, who may have lent money to their predecessors, beyond their faculties of paying.

What is true of generations succeeding one another at fixed epochs, as has been supposed for clearer conception, is true for those renewed daily, as in the actual course of nature. As a majority of the contracting generation will continue in being thirty-four years, and a new majority will then come into possession, the former may extend their engagement to that term, and no longer. The conclusion then, is, that neither the representatives of a nation, nor the whole nation itself assembled, can validly engage debts beyond what they may pay in their own time, that is to say, within thirty-four years of the date of the engagement.

Two laws of finance to be followed
To L. Williams, 1820: N. Y. Pub. Lib., MS, IV, 486

With respect to debts, whether to be met by loans or taxes, there are two laws of finance which I think should be rigorously adhered to. 1, never to borrow without laying a tax sufficient to pay principal and interest within a fixed period, and I would fix that period at 10 years . . . 2, never to borrow or tax without appropriating the money to its specific object.

Public debt leads to misery and decay
To Gallatin, 1809

I consider the fortunes of our republic as depending . . . on the extinguishment of the public debt before we engage in any war. . . . If the debt should once more be swelled to a formidable size, its entire discharge will be despaired of, and we shall be committed to the English career of debt, corruption and rottenness, closing with revolution.

To S. Kercheval, 1816

I am not among those who fear the people. They, and not the rich, are our dependence for continued freedom. And to preserve their independence, we must not let our rulers load us with perpetual debt. We must make our election between *economy and liberty,* or *profusion and servitude.* If we run into such debts, as that we must be taxed in our meat and in our drink, in our necessaries and our comforts, in our labors and our amusements, for our callings and our creeds, as the people of England are, our people, like them, must come to labor sixteen hours in the twenty-four, give the earnings of fifteen of these to the government for their debts and daily expenses; and the sixteenth being insufficient to afford us bread, we must live, as they now do, on oatmeal and potatoes; have no time to think, no means of calling the mismanagers to account; but be glad to obtain subsistence by hiring ourselves to rivet their chains on the necks of our fellow-sufferers. Our land-holders, too, like theirs, retaining indeed the title and stewardship of estates called theirs, but held really in trust for the treasury, must wander, like theirs, in foreign countries, and be contented with penury, obscurity, exile, and the glory of the nation. This example reads to us the salutary lesson, that private fortunes are destroyed by public as well as by private extravagance. And this is the tendency of all human governments. A departure from principle in one instance becomes a precedent for a second; that second for a third; and so on, till the bulk of the society is reduced to mere automatons of misery, to have no sensibilities left but for sinning and suffering. Then begins, indeed, the *bellum omnium in omnia,* which some philosophers observing to be so general in this world, have mistaken it for the natural, instead of the abusive state of man. And the fore horse of this frightful team is public debt. Taxation follows that, and in its train wretchedness and oppression.

III. Taxation

Taxation necessary for defense
To Washington, 1788

Calculation has convinced me that circumstances may arise, and probably will arise, wherein all the resources of taxation will be necessary for the safety of the State. For though I am decidedly of opinion we should take no part in European quarrels, but cultivate peace and commerce with all, yet who can avoid seeing the source of war, in the tyranny of those nations, who deprive us of the natural right of trading with our neighbors? The produce of the United States will soon exceed the European demand; what is to be done with the surplus, when there shall be one? It will be employed, without question, to open, by force, a market for itself, with those placed on the same continent with us, and who wish nothing better. Other causes, too, are obvious, which may involve us in war; and war requires every resource of taxation and credit.

Government to exercise rigorous economy
First Annual Message, December 8, 1801

Considering the general tendency to multiply offices and dependencies, and to increase expense to the ultimate term of burden which the citizen can bear, it behooves us to avail ourselves of every occasion which presents itself for taking off the surcharge; that it never may be seen here that, after leaving to labor the smallest portion of its earnings on which it can subsist, government shall itself consume the residue of what it was instituted to guard.

Desirability of an annual public budget
To Gallatin, 1804: N. Y. Pub. Lib., MS, II, 476

Would it not be useful also to oblige our successors, by setting the example ourselves, of laying annually before Congress a calendar of the expenditures: 1 for the civil, 2 the military, 3 the naval departments, in a single sum each? The greatest security against the introduction of corrupt practices and principles into our government, which can be relied on in practice, is to make the continuance of an administration depend on their keeping the public expenses down to their minimum. The people at large are not judges of theoretic principles, but they can judge on comparative statements of expense of different epochs.

Constant public control over tax-enactments
To—(?), 1813: N. Y. Pub. Lib., MS, IV, 190

Taxes should be continued by annual or biennial re-enactments; because a constant hold by the nation of the strings of the public purse is a salutary restraint from which an honest government ought not to wish, nor a corrupt one to be permitted to be free.

Taxation of the rich for the benefit of the poor
To Dupont de Nemours, 1811

We are all the more reconciled to the tax on importations, because it falls exclusively on the rich. . . . In fact, the poor man in this country who uses nothing but what is made within his own farm or family, or within the United States, pays not a farthing of tax to the general government, but on his salt; and should we go into that manufacture as we ought to do, we will pay not one cent. Our revenues once liberated by the discharge of the public debt, and its surplus applied to canals, roads, schools, etc., and the farmer will see his government supported, his children educated, and the face of the country made a paradise by the contributions of the rich alone, without his being called on to spare a cent from his earnings. The path we are now pursuing leads directly to this end.

To Kosciuszko, 1811

However, therefore, we may have been reproached for pursuing our Quaker system, time will affix the stamp of wisdom on it, and the happiness and prosperity of our citizens will attest its merit. And this, I believe, is the only legitimate object of government, and the first duty of governors, and not the slaughter of men and devastation of the countries placed under their care, in pursuit of a fantastic honor, unallied to virtue or happiness; or in gratification of the angry passions, or the pride of administrators, excited by personal incidents, in which their citizens have no concern.

IV. Banking

Danger of a monopolistic bank
To Gallatin, 1803

This institution [Bank of the United States] is one of the most deadly hostility existing, against the principles and form of our Constitution. The nation is, at this time . . . , strong and united. . . . But suppose a series of untoward events should occur, sufficient to bring into doubt the competency of a republican government to meet a crisis of great danger, or to unhinge the confidence of the people in the public functionaries; an institution like this, penetrating by its branches every part of the Union, acting by command and in phalanx, may, in a critical moment, upset the government. I deem no government safe which is under the vassalage of any self-constituted authorities, or any other authority than that of the nation. . . .

What an obstruction could not this bank of the United

States, with all its branch banks, be in time of war? It might dictate to us the peace we should accept, or withdraw its aids. Ought we then to give further growth to an institution so powerful, so hostile? . . . Now, while we are strong, it is the greatest duty we owe to the safety of our Constitution, to bring this powerful enemy to a perfect subordination under its authorities.

To Gallatin, 1802

The monopoly of a single bank is certainly an evil.

Small cash-banks are preferable to big discount ones
To J. W. Eppes, 1813

But it will be asked, are we to have no banks? Are merchants and others to be deprived of the resources of short accommodations, found so convenient? I answer, let us have banks; but let them be such as are alone to be found in any country on earth, except Great Britain. There is not a bank of discount on the continent of Europe, (at least there was not one when I was there), which offers anything but cash in exchange for discounted bills. No one has a natural right to the trade of a money lender, but he who has the money to lend. Let those then among us, who have a monied capital, and who prefer employing it in loans rather than otherwise, set up banks, and give cash or national bills for the notes they discount. Perhaps, to encourage them, a larger interest than is legal in the other cases might be allowed them, on the condition of their lending for short periods only.

Menace of the speculation mania
To Dr. T. Cooper, 1814

We are to be ruined now by the deluge of bank paper, as we were formerly by the old Continental paper. It is cruel that such revolutions in private fortunes should be at the mercy of avaricious adventurers, who, instead of employing their capital, if any they have, in manufactures, commerce, and other useful pursuits, make it an instrument to burthen all the interchanges of property with their swindling profits, profits which are the price of no useful industry of theirs. Prudent men must be on their guard in this game of *Robin's alive,* and take care that the spark does not extinguish in their hands. I am an enemy to all banks discounting bills or notes for anything but coin. But our whole country is so fascinated

To Gallatin, 1815

We are undone . . . if this banking mania be not suppressed. *Aut Carthago, aut Roma delenda est.** The war, had it proceeded, would have upset our government; and a new one, whenever tried, will do it. And so it must be while our money, the nerve of war, is much or little, real or imaginary, as our bitterest enemies choose to make it. Put down the banks, and if this country could not be carried through the longest war against her most powerful enemy, without ever knowing the want of a dollar, without dependence on the traitorous classes of her citizens, without bearing hard on the resources of the people, or loading the public with an indefinite burthen of debt, I know nothing of my countrymen. Not by any novel project, not by any charlatenerie, but by ordinary and well-experienced means; by the total prohibition of all private paper at all times, by reasonable taxes in war aided by the necessary emissions of public paper of circulating size, this bottomed on special taxes, redeemable annually as this special tax comes in.

The crazy bank bubble will explode
To Colonel Yancey, 1816

Like a dropsical man calling out for water, water, our deluded citizens are clamoring for more banks, more banks. The American mind is now in that state of fever which the world has so often seen in the history of other nations. We are under the bank bubble, as England was under the South Sea bubble, France under the Mississippi bubble, and as every nation is liable to be, under whatever bubble, design, or delusion may puff up in moments when off their guard. We are now taught to believe that legerdemain tricks upon paper can produce as solid wealth as hard labor in the earth. It is vain for common sense to urge that *nothing* can produce but *nothing;* that it is an idle dream to believe in a philosopher's stone which is to turn everything into gold, and to redeem man from the original sentence of his Maker, "in the sweat of his brow shall he eat his bread." Not Quixot enough, however, to attempt to reason Bedlam to rights, my anxieties are turned to the most practicable means of withdrawing us from the ruin into which we have run. Two hundred millions

* Either Carthage or Rome must be destroyed.

of paper in the hands of the people . . . is a fearful tax to fall at haphazard on their heads. The debt which purchased our independence was but of eighty millions, of which twenty years of taxation had in 1809 paid but the one half. And what have we purchased with this tax of two hundred millions which we are to pay by wholesale but usury, swindling, and new forms of demoralization. Revolutionary history has warned us of the probable moment when this baseless trash is to receive its fiat. Whenever so much of the precious metals shall have turned into the circulation as that every one can get some in exchange for his produce, paper, as in the revolutionary war, will experience at once an universal rejection.

A monied aristocracy threatens the republic
   To Dr. J. B. Stuart, 1817

Her [England's] examples have fearful influence on us. In copying her we do not seem to consider that like premises induce like consequences. The bank mania is one of the most threatening of these imitations. It is raising up a monied aristocracy in our country which has already set the government at defiance, and although forced at length to yield a little on this first essay of their strength, their principles are unyielded and unyielding. These have taken deep root in the hearts of that class from which our legislators are drawn, and the sop to Cerberus from fable has become history. Their principles lay hold of the good, their pelf of the bad, and thus those whom the constitution had placed as guards to its portals, are sophisticated or suborned from their duties. That paper money has some advantages, is admitted. But that its abuses also are inevitable, and, by breaking up the measure of value, makes a lottery of all private property, cannot be denied. Shall we ever be able to put a constitutional veto on it?

CHAPTER V

SOCIAL WELFARE

I. Classes

Uselessness of idle aristocrats
   To De Meunier, 1786

AN INDUSTRIOUS farmer occupies a more dignified place in the scale of beings . . . than a lazy lounger, valuing himself on his family, too proud to work, and drawing out a miserable existence by eating on that surplus of other men's labor, which is the sacred fund of the helpless poor.

Cincinnati Society may lead to hereditary caste
To Washington, 1784

The objections of those who are opposed to the institution [Cincinnati Society] shall be briefly sketched. You will readily fill them up. They urge that it is against the Confederation—against the letter of some of our constitutions—against the spirit of all of them;—that the foundation on which all these are built, is the natural equality of man, the denial of every preëminence but that annexed to legal office, and, particularly, the denial of a preëminence by birth; that, however, in their present dispositions, citizens might decline accepting honorary instalments into the order, a time may come, when a change of dispositions would render these flattering, when a well-directed distribution of them might draw into the order all the men of talents, of office and wealth, and in this case, would probably procure an ingraftment into the government; that in this, they will be supported by their foreign members, and the wishes and influence of foreign courts; that experience has shown that the hereditary branches of modern governments are the patrons of privilege and prerogative, and not of the natural rights of the people, whose oppressors they generally are; that, besides these evils, which are remote, others may take place more immediately; that a distinction is kept up between the civil and military, which it is for the happiness of both to obliterate; that when the members assemble they will be proposing to do something, and what that something may be, will depend on actual circumstances; that being an organized body, under habits of subordination, the first obstruction to enterprise will be already surmounted; that the moderation and virtue of a single character have probably prevented this Revolution from being closed, as most others have been, by a subversion of that liberty it was intended to establish; that he is not immortal, and his successor, or some of his successors, may be led by false calculation into a less certain road to glory.

To Washington, 1786

What has heretofore passed between us on this institution, makes it my duty to mention to you, that I have never heard a person in Europe, learned or unlearned, express his thoughts on this institution, who did not consider it as dishonorable and destructive to our governments; and that every writing which has come out since my arrival here, in which it is mentioned, considers it, even as now reformed, as the germ whose development is one day to destroy the fabric we have reared. I did not apprehend this, while I had American ideas only. But I confess that what I have seen in Europe has brought me over to that opinion; and that though the day may be at some distance, beyond the reach of our lives perhaps, yet it will certainly come, when a single fiber left of this institution will produce an hereditary aristocracy, which will change the form of our governments from the best to the worst in the world. To know the mass of evil which flows from this fatal source, a person must be in France; he must see the finest soil, the finest climate, the most compact State, the most benevolent character of people, and every earthly advantage combined, insufficient to prevent this scourge from rendering existence a curse to twenty-four out of twenty-five parts of the inhabitants of this country. With us, the branches of this institution cover all the States. The southern ones, at this time, are aristocratical in their dispositions; and, that that spirit should grow and extend itself, is within the natural order of things. I do not flatter myself with the immortality of our governments; but I shall think little also of their longevity, unless this germ of destruction be taken out. When the society themselves shall weigh the possibility of evil, against the impossibility of any good to proceed from this institution, I cannot help hoping they will eradicate it. I know they wish the permanence of our governments, as much as any individuals composing them.

No class distinction in America
To De Meunier, 1786

It should be further considered, that in America no other distinction between man and man had ever been known, but that of persons in office, exercising powers by authority of the laws, and private individuals. Among these last, the poorest laborer stood on equal ground with the wealthiest millionaire, and generally on a more favored one, whenever their rights seemed to jar. It has been seen that a shoemaker or other artisan, removed by the voice of his country from his work bench into a chair of office, has instantly commanded all the respect and obedience which the laws ascribe to his office. But of distinction by birth or badge, they had no more idea than they had of the mode of existence in the moon or planets. They had heard only that there were such, and knew that they must be wrong. A due horror of the evils which flow from these distinctions, could be excited in Europe only, where the dignity of man is lost in arbitrary distinctions, where the human species is classed into several stages of degradation, where the many are crushed under the weight of the few, and where the order established, can present to the contemplation of a thinking being, no other picture than that of God Almighty and his angels, trampling under foot the host of the damned.

Europe's class system is doomed
To Adams, 1813

But even in Europe a change has sensibly taken place in the minds of men. Science has liberated the ideas of those who read and reflect, and the American example has kindled feelings of right in the people. An insurrection has consequently begun of science, talents and courage, against rank and birth, which have fallen into contempt. It has failed in its first effort. . . . But the world will soon recover from the panic of this first catastrophe. Science is progressive, and talents and enterprise are on the alert. . . . Rank and birth, and tinsel-aristocracy will finally shrink into insignificance.

Natural versus artificial aristocracy
To Adams, 1813

For I agree . . . that there is a natural aristocracy among men. The grounds of this are virtue and talents. Formerly, bodily powers gave place among the aristoi. But since the invention of gunpowder has armed the weak as well as the strong with missile death, bodily strength, like beauty, good humor, politeness and other accomplishments, has become but an auxiliary ground of distinction. There is also an artificial aristocracy, founded on wealth and birth, without either virtue or talents; for with these it would belong to the first class. The natural aristocracy I consider as the most precious gift of nature, for the instruction, the trusts, and government of society. . . .

May we not even say, that that form of government is best, which provides the most effectually for a pure selection of these natural aristoi into the offices of government? The artificial aristocracy is a mischievous ingredient in government, and provision should be made to prevent its ascendancy. . . . I think the best remedy is exactly that provided by all our constitutions, to leave to the citizens the free election and separation of the aristoi from the pseudo-aristoi, of the wheat from the chaff. In general they will elect the really good and wise. In some instances, wealth may corrupt, and birth blind them; but not in sufficient degree to endanger the society. . . .

At the first session of our legislature after the Declaration of Independence, we passed a law abolishing entails. And this was followed by one abolishing the privilege of primogeniture, and dividing the lands of intestates equally among all their children. . . . These laws, drawn by myself, laid the ax to the foot of pseudo-aristocracy. And had another which I prepared been adopted by the legislature, our work would have been complete. It was a bill for the more general diffusion of learning. This proposed to divide every county into wards of five or six miles square . . .; to establish in each ward a free school for reading, writing and common arithmetic; to provide for the annual selection of the best subjects from these schools, who might receive, at the public expense, a higher degree of education at a district school; and from these district schools to select a certain number of the most promising subjects, to be completed at an University, where all the useful sciences should be taught. Worth and genius would thus have been sought out from every condition of life, and completely prepared by education for defeating the competition of wealth and birth for public trusts. . . . Although this law has not yet been acted on . . . , I have great hope that some patriotic spirit will, at a favorable moment, call it up, and make it the keystone of the arch of our government.

With respect to aristocracy, we should further consider, that before the establishment of the American States, nothing was known to history but the man of the old world, crowded within limits either small or overcharged, and steeped in the vices which that situation generates. A government adapted to such men would be one thing; but a very different one, that for the man of these States. Here every one may have land to labor for himself, if he chooses; or, preferring the exercise of any other industry, may exact for it such compensation as not only to afford a comfortable subsistence, but wherewith to provide for a cessation from labor in old age.

Every one, by his property or by his satisfactory situation, is interested in the support of law and order. And such men may safely and advantageously reserve to themselves a wholesome control over their public affairs, and a degree of freedom which, in the hands of the *canaille* of the cities of Europe, would be instantly perverted to the demolition and destruction of everything public and private.

Massachusetts, too, will abolish the class system
To Welles, 1819: N. Y. Pub. Lib., MS, V, 125

Of the return of Massachusetts to sound principles I never had a doubt. The body of her citizens has never been otherwise than republican. Her would-be dukes and lords indeed, have been itching for coronets; her lawyers for robes of ermin, her priests for lawn sleeves, and for a religious establishment which might give them wealth, power, and independence of personal merit. But her citizens who were to supply with the sweat of their brow the treasures on which these drones were to riot, could never have seen anything to long for in the oppressions and pauperism of England. After the shackles of Autocracy of the bar and priesthood have been burnt by Connecticut, we cannot doubt the return of Massachusetts to the bosom of the republican family.

American farmers, a barrier against a class system
To H. G. Spafford, 1814

I join in your reprobation of our merchants, priests, and lawyers for their adherence to England and monarchy, in preference to their own country and its constitution. But merchants have no country. The mere spot they stand on does not constitute so strong an attachment as that from which they draw their gains. In every country and in every age, the priest has been hostile to liberty. He is always in alliance with the despot, abetting his abuses in return for protection to his own. It is easier to acquire wealth and power by this combination than by deserving them, and to effect this, they have perverted the purest religion ever preached to man into mystery and jargon, unintelligible to all mankind, and therefore the safer engine for their purposes.

With the lawyers it is a new thing. They have, in the mother country, been generally the firmest supporters of the free principles of their constitution. But there too they have changed. I ascribe much of this to the substitution of Blackstone for my Lord Coke, as an elementary work. In truth,

SOCIAL WELFARE

Blackstone and Hume have made tories of all England, and are making tories of those young Americans whose native feelings of independence do not place them above the wily sophistries of a Hume or a Blackstone. These two books, but especially the former, have done more towards the suppression of the liberties of man, than all the million of men in arms of Bonaparte and the millions of human lives with the sacrifice of which he will stand loaded before the judgment seat of his Maker.

I fear nothing for our liberty from the assaults of force; but I have seen and felt much, and fear more from English books, English prejudices, English manners, and the apes, the dupes, and designs among our professional crafts. When I look around me for security against these seductions, I find it in the widespread of our agricultural citizens, in their unsophisticated minds, their independence and their power, if called on, to crush the Humists of our cities, and to maintain the principles which severed us from England.

Happy state of American workers, compared to English
To T. Cooper, 1814

The great mass of our population is of laborers; our rich, who can live without labor, either manual or professional, being few, and of moderate wealth. Most of the laboring class possess property, cultivate their own lands, have families, and from the demand for their labor are enabled to exact from the rich and the competent such prices as enable them to be fed abundantly, clothed above mere decency, to labor moderately and raise their families. They are not driven to the ultimate resources of dexterity and skill, because their wares will sell although not quite so nice as those of England.

The wealthy, on the other hand, and those at their ease, know nothing of what the Europeans call luxury. They have only somewhat more of the comforts and decencies of life than those who furnish them. Can any condition of society be more desirable than this?

Nor in the class of laborers do I mean to withhold from the comparison that portion whose color has condemned them, in certain parts of our Union, to a subjection to the will of others. Even these are better fed in these States, warmer clothed, and labor less than the journeymen or day-laborers of England. They have the comfort, too, of numerous families, in the midst of whom they live without want, or fear of it; a solace which few of the laborers of England possess. They are subject, it is true, to bodily coercion; but are not the hundreds of thousands of British soldiers and seamen subject to the same, without seeing, at the end of their career, when age and accident shall have rendered them unequal to labor, the certainty, which the other has, that he will never want? And has not the British seaman, as much as the African, been reduced to this bondage by force, in flagrant violation of his own consent, and of his natural right in his own person? and with the laborers of England generally, does not the moral coercion of want subject their will as despotically to that of their employer, as the physical constraint does the soldier, the seaman, or the slave? But do not mistake me. I am not advocating slavery. I am not justifying the wrongs we have committed on a foreign people, by the example of another nation committing equal wrongs on their own subjects. On the contrary, there is nothing I would not sacrifice to a practicable plan of abolishing every vestige of this moral and political depravity. But I am at present comparing the condition and degree of suffering to which oppression has reduced the man of one color, with the condition and degree of suffering to which oppression has reduced the man of another color; equally condemning both.

Now let us compute by numbers the sum of happiness of the two countries. In England, happiness is the lot of the aristocracy only; and the proportion they bear to the laborers and paupers, you know better than I do. Were I to guess that they are four in every hundred, then the happiness of the nation would be to its misery as one in twenty-five. In the United States it is as eight millions to zero, or as all to none. But it said they possess the means of defense, and that we do not. How so? Are we not men? Yes; but our men are so happy at home that they will not hire themselves to be shot at for a shilling a day. Hence we can have no standing armies for defense, because we have no paupers to furnish the materials. The Greeks and Romans had no standing armies, yet they defended themselves. The Greeks by their laws, and the Romans by the spirit of their people, took care to put into the hands of their rulers no such engine of oppression as a standing army. Their system was to make every man a soldier, and oblige him to repair to the standard of his country whenever that was reared. This made them invincible; and the same remedy will make us so.

II. Education

Only popular education can safeguard democracy
Notes on Virginia, Query 14

In every government on earth is some trace of human weakness, some germ of corruption and degeneracy, which cunning will discover, and wickedness insensibly open, cultivate and improve. Every government degenerates when trusted to the rulers of the people alone. The people themselves are its only safe depositories. And to render even them safe, their minds must be improved to a certain degree. . . . An amendment of our constitution must here come in aid of the public education. The influence over government must be shared among all the people. If every individual . . . participates of the ultimate authority, the government will be safe.

To Wythe, 1786

I think by far the most important bill in our whole code, is that for the diffusion of knowledge among the people. No other sure foundation can be devised, for the preservation of freedom and happiness. If anybody thinks that kings, nobles, or priests are good conservators of the public happiness, send him here [to Paris]. It is the best school in the universe to cure him of that folly. He will see here, with his own eyes, that these descriptions of men are an abandoned confederacy against the happiness of the mass of the people. The omnipotence of their effect cannot be better proved, than in this country particularly, where, notwithstanding the finest soil upon earth, the finest climate under heaven, and a people of the most benevolent, the most gay and amiable character of which the human form is susceptible; where such a people, I say, surrounded by so many blessings from nature, are loaded with misery, by kings, nobles, and priests, and by them alone. Preach, my dear Sir, a crusade against ignorance; establish and improve the law for educating the common people. Let our countrymen know, that the people alone can protect us against these evils, and that the tax which will be paid for this purpose, is not more than the thousandth part of what will be paid to kings, priests and nobles, who will rise up among us if we leave the people in ignorance. The people of England, I think, are less oppressed than here. But it needs but half an eye to see, when among them, that the foundation is laid in their dispositions for the establishment of a despotism. Nobility, wealth, and pomp, are the objects of their admiration. They are by no means the free-minded people we suppose them in America. Their learned men, too, are few in number, and are less learned, and infinitely less emancipated from prejudice, than those of this country.

To Price, 1789

A sense of necessity, and a submission to it, is to me a new and consolatory proof that, whenever the people are well-informed, they can be trusted with their own government; that, whenever things get so far wrong as to attract their notice, they may be relied on to set them to rights.

Education for agricultural skill
To David Williams, 1803

The greatest evils of populous society have ever appeared to me to spring from the vicious distribution of its members among the occupations called for. I have no doubt that those nations are essentially right, which leave this to individual choice, as a better guide to an advantageous distribution. . . . But when, by a blind concourse, particular occupations are ruinously overcharged, and others left in want of hands, the national authorities can do much towards restoring the equilibrium.

On the revival of letters,* learning became the universal favorite. And with reason, because there was not enough of it existing to manage the affairs of a nation to the best advantage, nor to advance its individuals to . . . happiness . . . , by improvements in their minds, their morals, their health, and in those conveniences which contribute to the comfort and embellishment of life. All the efforts of the society, therefore, were directed to the increase of learning, and the inducements of respect, ease, and profit were held up for its encouragement. Even the charities of the nation forgot that misery was their object, and spent themselves in founding schools to transfer to science the hardy sons of the plow. To these incitements were added the powerful fascinations of great cities.

These circumstances have long since produced an overcharge in the class of competitors for learned occupation, and great distress among the supernumerary candidates; and the more, as their habits of life have disqualified them for re-entering into the laborious class. The evil cannot be suddenly, nor perhaps ever entirely cured. . . . Doubtless there

* The reference is to the Italian Renascence.

are many engines which the nation might bring to bear on this object. Public opinion, and public encouragement are among these.

The class principally defective is that of agriculture. It is the first in utility, and ought to be the first in respect. The same artificial means which have been used to produce a competition in learning, may be equally successful in restoring agriculture to its primary dignity in the eyes of men. It is a science of the very first order. It counts among its handmaids the most respectable sciences, such as Chemistry, Natural Philosophy, Mechanics, Mathematics, Natural History, Botany. In every College and University, a professorship of agriculture, and the class of its students, might be honored as the first. Young men closing their academical education with this, as the crown of all other sciences . . . , instead of crowding the other classes, would return to the farms of their fathers, their own, or those of others, and replenish and invigorate a calling, now languishing under contempt and oppression. The charitable schools, instead of storing their pupils with a lore which the present state of society does not call for, converted into schools of agriculture, might restore them to that branch qualified to enrich and honor themselves, and to increase the productions of the nation instead of consuming them. A gradual abolition of the useless offices so much accumulated in all governments, might close this drain also from the labors of the field, and lessen the burthens imposed on them. By these . . . means . . . the sum of industry [will] be increased, and that of misery diminished.

Ignorant people can not maintain their freedom
To Colonel Yancey, 1816

If a nation expects to be ignorant and free, in a state of civilization, it expects what never was and never will be. The functionaries of every government have propensities to command at will the liberty and property of their constituents. There is no safe deposit for these but with the people themselves; nor can they be safe with them without information. Where the press is free, and every man able to read, all is safe.

To Jarvis, 1821

I know of no safe depository of the ultimate powers of the society but the people themselves; and if we think them not enlightened enough to exercise their control with a wholesome discretion, the remedy is not to take it from them, but to inform their discretion by education.

Education need not be compulsory
Plan for Elementary Schools, September, 1817

Is it a right or a duty in society to take care of their infant members in opposition to the will of the parent? How far does this right and duty extend?—to guard the life of the infant, his property, his instructions, his morals? The Roman father was supreme in all these: we draw a line, but where?—public sentiment does not seem to have traced it precisely. Nor is it necessary in the present case. It is better to tolerate the rare instance of a parent refusing to let his child be educated, than to shock the common feelings and ideas by the forcible asportation and education of the infant against the will of the father.

Progress in knowledge will lead to human happiness
To Dr. Waterhouse, 1818

When I contemplate the immense advances in science and discoveries in the arts which have been made within the period of my life, I look forward with confidence to equal advances by the present generation, and have no doubt they will consequently be as much wiser than we have been as we than our fathers were, and they than the burners of witches.

To—(?), 1821

Science is more important in a republican than in any other government. And in an infant country like ours, we must much depend for improvement on the science of other countries, longer established, possessing better means, and more advanced than we are. To prohibit us from the benefit of foreign light, is to consign us to long darkness.

Why send American youth to Europe for education?
To Bannister, Jr., 1785

But why send an American youth to Europe for education? What are the objects of an useful American education? Classical knowledge, modern languages, chiefly French, Spanish, and Italian; Mathematics, Natural philosophy, Natural history, Civil history, and Ethics. In Natural philosophy, I mean to include Chemistry and Agriculture, and in Natural history, to include Botany, as well as the other branches of those departments. It is true that the habit of speaking the modern languages cannot be so well acquired in America; but every other article can be as well acquired at William and Mary college as at any place in Europe. When college education is done with, and a young man is to prepare himself for public life, he must cast his eyes (for America) either on Law or Physics. For the former, where can he apply so advantageously as to Mr. Wythe? For the latter, he must come to Europe: the medical class of students, therefore, is the only one which need come to Europe.

Let us view the disadvantages of sending a youth to Europe. To enumerate them all, would require a volume. I will select a few. If he goes to England, he learns drinking, horse racing, and boxing. These are the peculiarities of English education. The following circumstances are common to education in that, and the other countries of Europe. He acquires a fondness for European luxury and dissipation, and a contempt for the simplicity of his own country; he is fascinated with the privileges of the European aristocrats, and sees, with abhorrence, the lovely equality which the poor enjoy with the rich, in his own country; he contracts a partiality for aristocracy or monarchy; he forms foreign friendships which will never be useful to him, and loses the seasons of life for forming, in his own country, those friendships which, of all others, are the most faithful and permanent; he is led, by the strongest of all the human passions, into a spirit for female intrigue, destructive of his own and others' happiness, or a passion for whores, destructive of his health, and, in both cases, learns to consider fidelity to the marriage bed as an ungentlemanly practice, and inconsistent with happiness; he recollects the voluptuary dress and arts of the European women, and pities and despises the chaste affections and simplicity of those of his own country; he retains, through life, a fond recollection, and a hankering after those places, which were the scenes of his first pleasures and his first connections; he returns to his own country, a foreigner, unacquainted with the practices of domestic economy, necessary to preserve him from ruin, speaking and writing his native tongue as a foreigner, and therefore unqualified to obtain those distinctions, which eloquence of the pen and tongue ensures in a free country; for I would observe to you, that what is called style in writing or speaking is formed very early in life, while the imagination is warm, and impressions are permanent. I am of the opinion, that there never was an instance of a man's writing or speaking his native tongue with elegance, who passed from fifteen to twenty years of age out of the country where it was spoken. Thus, no instance exists of a person's writing two languages perfectly. That will always appear to be his native language, which was most familiar to him in his youth. It appears to me, then, that an American, coming to Europe for education, loses in his knowledge, in his morals, in his health, in his habits, and in his happiness. I had entertained only doubts on this head before I came to Europe: what I see and hear, since I came here, proves more than I had even suspected. Cast your eye over America: who are the men of most learning, of most eloquence, most beloved by their countrymen and most trusted and promoted by them? They are those who have been educated among them, and whose manners, morals, and habits, are perfectly homogeneous with those of the country.

Happiness of man lies in popular education
To C. C. Blatchly, 1822

I look to the diffusion of light and education as the resource most to be relied on for ameliorating the condition, promoting the virtue, and advancing the happiness of man. That every man shall be made virtuous, by any process whatever, is, indeed, no more to be expected, than that every tree shall be made to bear fruit, and every plant nourishment. The brier and bramble can never become the vine and olive; but their asperities may be softened by culture, and their properties improved to usefulness in the order and economy of the world. And I do hope that, in the present spirit of extending to the great mass of mankind the blessings of instruction, I see a prospect of great advancement in the happiness of the human race; and that this may proceed to an indefinite, although not to an infinite degree.

III. Press

A free press is the only safeguard of public liberty
To Carrington, 1787

I am persuaded myself that the good sense of the people will always be found to be the best army. They may be led astray for a moment, but will soon correct themselves. The people are the only censors of their governors; and even their errors will tend to keep these to the true principles of their institution. To punish these errors too severely would be to suppress the only safeguard of the public liberty. The way to prevent these irregular interpositions of the people, is to give them full information of their affairs through the channel of the public papers, and to contrive that those papers should penetrate the whole mass of the people. The basis of our governments being the opinion of the people, the very first object should be to keep that right; and were it left to me to decide whether we should have a government without newspapers, or newspapers without a government, I should not hesitate a moment to prefer the latter. But I should mean that every man should receive those papers, and be capable of reading them. I am convinced that those societies (as the Indians) which live without government, enjoy in their general mass an infinitely greater degree of happiness than those who live under the European governments. Among the former, public opinion is in the place of law, and restrains morals as powerfully as laws ever did anywhere. Among the latter, under pretense of governing, they have divided their nations into two classes, wolves and sheep. I do not exaggerate. This is a true picture of Europe. Cherish, therefore, the spirit of our people, and keep alive their attention. Do not be too severe upon their errors, but reclaim them by enlightening them. If once they become inattentive to the public affairs, you and I, and Congress and Assemblies, Judges and Governors, shall all become wolves. It seems to be the law of our general nature, in spite of individual exceptions; and experience declares that man is the only animal which devours his own kind; for I can apply no milder term to the governments of Europe, and to the general prey of the rich on the poor.

To Washington, 1792

No government ought to be without censors; and where the press is free, no one ever will. If virtuous, it need not fear the fair operation of attack and defense. Nature has given to man no other means of sifting out the truth, either in religion, law, or politics.

A free press is the triumph of humanity over oppression
Virginia and Kentucky Resolutions, 1799*

In every State, probably, in the Union, the press has exerted a freedom in canvassing the merits and measures of public men, of every description, which has not been confined to the strict limits of the common law . . . Some degree of abuse is

* Madison was part author of this.

inseparable from the proper use of every thing; and in no instance is this more true, than in that of the press. It has accordingly been decided by the practice of the States, that it is better to leave a few of its noxious branches, to their luxuriant growth, than by pruning them away, to injure the vigor of those yielding the proper fruits. And can the wisdom of this policy be doubted by any who reflect, that to the press alone, chequered as it is with abuses, the world is indebted for all the triumphs which have been gained by reason and humanity, over error and oppression; who reflect, that to the same beneficent source, the United States owe much of the lights which conducted them to the rank of a free and independent nation; and which have improved their political system into a shape so auspicious to their happiness. Had 'Sedition Acts', forbidding every publication that might bring the constituted agents into contempt or disrepute, or that might excite the hatred of the people against the authors of unjust or pernicious measures, been uniformly enforced against the press; might not the United States have been languishing at this day, under the infirmities of a sickly confederation: might they not possibly be miserable colonies, groaning under a foreign yoke?

But the press lends itself to incitement
To Elbridge Gerry, 1801

A coalition of sentiments is not for the interest of the printers. They, like the clergy, live by the zeal they can kindle, and the schisms they can create. It is contest of opinion in politics as well as religion which makes us take great interest in them, and bestow our money liberally on those who furnish ailment to our appetite. . . . So the printers can never leave us in a state of perfect rest and union of opinion. They would be no longer useful, and would have to go to the plow.

To Pictet, 1803

Indeed the abuses of the freedom of the press here have been carried to a length never before known or borne by any civilized nation. But it is so difficult to draw a clear line of separation between the abuse and the wholesome use of the press, that as yet we have found it better to trust the public judgment, rather than the magistrate, with the discrimination between truth and falsehood. And hitherto the public judgment has performed that office with wonderful correctness.

An experiment in toleration
To Volney, 1802: N. Y. Pub. Lib., MS, II, 199

They [Federalists] fill their newspapers with falsehoods, calumnies, and audacities. . . . We are going fairly through the experiment whether freedom of discussion, unaided by coercion, is not sufficient for the propagation and protection of truth, and for the maintenance of an administration pure and upright in its actions and views. No one ought to feel, under this experiment, more than myself. Nero wished all the necks of Rome united in one, that he might sever them at a blow. So our ex-federalists, wishing to have a single representative of all the objects of their hatred, honor me with that post, and exhibit against me such atrocities as no nation has ever before heard or endured. I shall protect them in the right of lying and caluminating, and still go on to merit the continuance of it, by pursuing steadily my object of proving that a people, easy in their circumstances as ours are, are capable of conducting themselves under a government founded not in the fears and follies of man, but on his reason, on the predominance of his social over his dissocial passions, so free as to restrain him in no moral right, and so firm as to protect him from every moral wrong, which shall leave him, in short, in possession of all his natural rights.

To Judge Tyler, 1804: N. Y. Pub. Lib., MS, III, 334

No experiment can be more interesting than that we are now trying, which we trust will end in establishing the fact that man may be governed by reason and truth. Our first object should therefore be to leave open to him all the avenues to truth. The most effectual hitherto found is the freedom of the press. It is therefore the first shut up by those who fear the investigation of their actions. The firmness with which the people have withstood the late abuses of the press, the discernment they have manifested between truth and falsehood shew that they may safely be trusted to hear everything true and false and to form a correct judgment between them. As little is it necessary to impose on their senses, or dazzle their minds by pomp, splendor or forms. Instead of this artificial, how much surer is the real respect which results from the use of their reason and the habit of bringing every thing to the test of common sense.

To Th. Seymour, 1807

I have lent myself willingly as the subject of a great experiment, which was to prove that an administration, conducting itself with integrity and common understanding, cannot be battered down, even by the falsehoods of a licentious press, and consequently still less by the press as restrained within the legal and wholesome limits of truth. This experiment was wanting for the world to demonstrate the falsehood of the pretext that freedom of the press is incompatible with orderly government. . . . [A true press] is a noble institution, equally the friend of science and of civil liberty.

Abuses of the press are regrettable, but must be borne
Second Inaugural, March 4, 1805

The artillery of the press has been leveled against us, charged with whatsoever its licentiousness could devise or dare. These abuses of an institution so important to freedom and science, are deeply to be regretted, inasmuch as they tend to lessen its usefulness, and to sap its safety; they might, indeed, have been corrected by the wholesome punishments reserved and provided by the laws of the several States against falsehood and defamation; but public duties more urgent press on the time of public servants, and the offenders have therefore been left to find their punishment in the public indignation.

Nor was it uninteresting to the world, that an experiment should be fairly and fully made, whether freedom of discussion, unaided by power, is not sufficient for the propagation and protection of truth—whether a government, conducting itself in the true spirit of its constitution, with zeal and purity, and doing no act which it would be unwilling the whole world should witness, can be written down by falsehood and defamation. The experiment has been tried; you have witnessed the scene; our fellow citizens have looked on, cool and collected; they saw the latent source from which these outrages proceeded; they gathered around their public functionaries, and when the constitution called them to the decision by suffrage, they pronounced their verdict, honorable to those who had served them, and consolatory to the friend of man, who believes he may be intrusted with his own affairs.

No inference is here intended, that the laws, provided by the State against false and defamatory publications, should not be enforced; he who has time, renders a service to public morals and public tranquillity, in reforming these abuses by the salutary coercions of the law; but the experiment is noted, to prove that, opinions in league with false facts, the press, confined to truth, needs no other legal restraint; the public judgment will correct false reasonings and opinions, on a full hearing of all parties; and no other definite line can be drawn between the inestimable liberty of the press and its demoralizing licentiousness. If there be still improprieties which this rule would not restrain, its supplement must be sought in the censorship of public opinion.

Lies of the press
To J. Norvell, 1807

It is a melancholy truth, that a suppression of the press could not more completely deprive the nation of its benefits, than is done by its abandoned prostitution to falsehood. Nothing can now be believed which is seen in a newspaper. Truth itself becomes suspicious by being put into that polluted vehicle. The real extent of this state of misinformation is known only to those who are in situations to confront facts within their knowledge with the lies of the day. I really look with commiseration over the great body of my fellow citizens, who, reading newspapers, live and die in the belief, that they have known something of what has been passing in the world in their time; whereas the accounts they have read in newspapers are just as true a history of any other period of the world as of the present, except that the real names of the day are affixed to their fables. General facts may indeed be collected from them, such as that Europe is now at war, that Bonaparte has been a successful warrior . . . , but no details can be relied on. I will add, that the man who never looks into a newspaper is better informed than he who reads them; inasmuch as he who knows nothing is nearer to truth than he whose mind is filled with falsehoods and errors. . . .

Perhaps an editor might begin a reformation in some such way as this. Divide his paper into four chapters, heading the 1st, Truths. 2d, Probabilities. 3d, Possibilities. 4th, Lies. The first chapter would be very short.

To Short, 1808

The papers have lately advanced in boldness and flagitiousness beyond even themselves. Such daring and atrocious lies as fill the third and fourth columns of the third page of the

United States Gazette of August 31st, were never, I believe, published with impunity in any country. However, I have from the beginning determined to submit myself as the subject on whom may be proved the impotency of a free press in a country like ours, against those who conduct themselves honestly and enter into no intrigue. I admit at the same time that restraining the press to *truth,* as the present laws do, is the only way of making it useful. But I have thought necessary first to prove it can never be dangerous.

To T. Wortman, 1813

Were I the publisher of a paper, instead of the usual division into Foreign, Domestic, etc., I think I should distribute everything under the following heads: 1. True. 2. Probable. 3. Wanting Confirmation. 4. Lies . . . At present it is disreputable to state a fact on newspaper authority; and the newspapers of our country by their abandoned spirit of falsehood, have more effectually destroyed the utility of the press than all the shackles devised by Bonaparte.

To Dr. D. W. Jones, 1814

I deplore . . . the putrid state into which our newspapers have passed, and the malignity, the vulgarity, and mendacious spirit of those who write them. . . . These ordures are rapidly depraving the public taste.

To Dr. J. Currie, 1786

It is however an evil for which there is no remedy, our liberty depends on the freedom of the press, and that cannot be limited without being lost.

IV. Minorities: Negroes

The evil effects of slavery on the masters
Notes on Virginia, Query 18

The whole commerce between master and slave is a perpetual exercise of the most boisterous passions, the most unremitting despotism on the one part, and degrading submissions on the other. Our children see this, and learn to imitate it; for man is an imitative animal. This quality is the germ of all education in him. From his cradle to his grave he is learning to do what he sees others do. If a parent could find no motive either in his philanthropy or his self-love, for restraining the intemperance of passion towards his slave, it should always be a sufficient one that his child is present. But generally it is not sufficient. The parent storms, the child looks on, catches the lineaments of wrath, puts on the same airs in the circle of smaller slaves, gives a loose to the worst of passions, and thus nursed, educated, and daily exercised in tyranny, cannot but be stamped by it with odious peculiarities. The man must be a prodigy who can retain his manners and morals undepraved by such circumstances.

And with what execration should the statesman be loaded, who, permitting one half the citizens thus to trample on the rights of the other, transforms those into despots, and these into enemies, destroys the morals of the one part, and the *amor patriæ* of the other. For if a slave can have a country in this world, it must be any other in preference to that in which he is born to live and labor for another; in which he must lock up the faculties of his nature, contribute as far as depends on his individual endeavors to the evanishment of the human race, or entail his own miserable condition on the endless generation proceeding from him.

With the morals of the people, their industry also is destroyed. For in a warm climate, no man will labor for himself who can make another labor for him. This is so true, that of the proprietors of slaves a very small proportion indeed are ever seen to labor. And can the liberties of a nation be thought secure when we have removed their only firm basis, a conviction in the minds of the people that these liberties are of the gift of God? That they are not to be violated but with his wrath? Indeed I tremble for my country when I reflect that God is just; that his justice cannot sleep forever.

Notes on Virginia, Query 14

And it is a problem which I give to the master to solve, whether the religious precepts against the violation of property were not framed for him as well as his slave? And whether the slave may not as justifiably take a little from one who has taken all from him, as he may slay one who would slay him? That a change in the relations in which a man is placed should change his ideas of moral right or wrong, is neither new, nor peculiar to the color of the blacks. Homer tells us it was so two thousand six hundred years ago.

> Jove fix'd it certain, that whatever day
> Makes a man a slave, takes half his worth away.

But the slaves of which Homer speaks were whites. Notwithstanding these considerations which must weaken their respect for the laws of property, we find among them numerous instances of the most rigid integrity, and as many as among their better instructed masters, of benevolence, gratitude, and unshaken fidelity. The opinion that they are inferior in the faculties of reason and imagination must be hazarded with great diffidence.

Hopes for the amelioration of the evil
To De Meunier, 1786

What a stupendous, what an incomprehensible machine is man! who can endure toil, famine, stripes, imprisonment, and death itself, in vindication of his own liberty, and, the next moment be deaf to all those motives whose power supported him through his trial, and inflict on his fellow men a bondage, one hour of which is fraught with more misery, than ages of that which he rose in rebellion to oppose. But we must await, with patience, the workings of an overruling Providence, and hope that that is preparing the deliverance of these, our suffering brethren. When the measure of their tears shall be full, when their groans shall have involved heaven itself in darkness, doubtless a God of justice will awaken to their distress.

Experiments in emancipation
To E. Bancroft, 1789

To give liberty to, or rather, to abandon persons whose habits have been formed in slavery is like abandoning children. Many Quakers in Virginia seated their slaves on their lands as tenants. . . . But . . . the landlord was obliged to plan their crops for them, to direct all their operations during every season and according to the weather. But what is more afflicting, he was obliged to watch them daily and almost constantly to make them work, and even to whip them. A man's moral sense must be unusually strong, if slavery does not make him a thief. He who is permitted by law to have no property of his own, can with difficulty conceive that property is founded in any thing but force . . .

Notwithstanding the discouraging result of these experiments, I am decided on my final return to America to try this one. I shall endeavor to import as many Germans as I have grown slaves. I will settle them and my slaves, on farms of 50 acres each, intermingled, and place all on the footing of the Metayers of Europe. Their children shall be brought up, as others are, in habits of property and foresight, & I have no doubt but that they will be good citizens.

Is it true that Negroes are inherently inferior?
To Banneker, 1791

No body wishes more than I do to see . . . proofs that nature has given to our black brethren, talents equal to those of the other colors of men, and that the appearance of a want of them is owing merely to the degraded condition of their existence, both in Africa and America. I can add with truth, that no body wishes more ardently to see a good system commenced for raising the condition both of their body & mind to what it ought to be, as fast as the imbecility of their present existence . . . will admit.

To Grégoire, 1809

No person living wishes more sincerely than I do, to see a complete refutation of the doubts I have myself entertained and expressed on the grade of understanding allotted to them [Negroes] by nature, and to find that in this respect they are on a par with ourselves. My doubts were the result of personal observation in the limited sphere of my own State, where the opportunities for the development of their genius were not favorable, and those of exercising it still less so. . . . But whatever be their degree of talent it is no measure of their rights. Because Sir Isaac Newton was superior to others in understanding, he was not therefore lord of the person or property of others.

Doubts as to the natural inferiority of Negroes
To Miss Wright, 1825

An opinion is hazarded by some, but proved by none, that moral urgencies are not sufficient to induce him [the man of color] to labor; that nothing can do this but physical coercion. But this is a problem which the present age alone is prepared to solve by experiment. It would be a solecism to suppose a race of animals created, without sufficient foresight and energy to preserve their own existence. It is disproved, too, by the fact that they exist, and have existed through all the ages of history. We are not sufficiently acquainted with all the nations of Africa, to say that there may not be some in which habits of industry are established, and the arts practiced which are necessary to render life comfortable. The experiment now in progress in St. Domingo, those of Sierra Leone and Cape Mesurado, are but beginning.

Fears of slave insurrection
To St. George Tucker, 1797

Whither shall the colored emigrants go? . . . If something is not done, and soon done, we shall be the murderers of our own children. . . . The revolutionary storm, now sweeping the globe, will be upon us, and happy if we make timely provision to give it an easy passage over our land. . . . The day which begins our combustion must be near at hand; and only a single spark is wanting to make that day to-morrow. If we had begun sooner, we might probably have been allowed a lengthier operation to clear ourselves, but every day's delay lessens the time we may take for emancipation.

Emigration of slaves to Africa?
To Dr. T. Humphreys, 1817

I concur entirely in your leading principles of gradual emancipation, of establishment on the coast of Africa, and the patronage of our nation until the emigrants shall be able to protect themselves. The subordinate details might be easily arranged. But the bare proposition of purchase by the United States generally, would excite infinite indignation in all the States north of Maryland. The sacrifice must fall on the States alone which hold them; and the difficult question will be how to lessen this so as to reconcile our fellow citizens to it. Personally I am ready and desirous to make any sacrifice which shall ensure their gradual but complete retirement from the States, and effectually, at the same time, establish them elsewhere in freedom and safety. But I have not perceived the growth of this disposition in the rising generation, of which I once had sanguine hopes. No symptoms inform me that it will take place in my day. I leave it, therefore, to time, and not at all without hope that the day will come, equally desirable and welcome to us as to them.

Gradual emancipation is more practicable than emigration
To Jared Sparks, 1824

To provide an asylum to which we can, by degrees, send the whole of that population [Negroes] from among us, and establish them under our patronage and protection, as a separate, free and independent people . . . on the coast of Africa . . . I have deemed entirely impossible. And without repeating the other arguments which have been urged by others, I will appeal to figures only. . . .

There are in the United States a million and a half of people of color in slavery. To send off the whole of these at once, nobody conceives to be practicable for us, or expedient for them. Let us take twenty-five years for its accomplishment, within which time they will be doubled. Their estimated value as property, in the first place, (for actual property has been lawfully vested in that form, and who can lawfully take it from the possessors?) at an average of two hundred dollars each, young and old, would amount to six hundred millions of dollars, which must be paid or lost by somebody. To this, add the cost of their transportation by land and sea to Mesurado, a year's provision of food and clothing, implements of husbandry and of their trades, which will amount to three hundred millions more, making thirty-six millions of dollars a year for twenty-five years, with insurance of peace all that time, and it is impossible to look at the question a second time. . . .

I do not say . . . that the getting rid of them is forever impossible. For that is neither my opinion nor my hope. But only that it cannot be done in this way. There is, I think, a way in which it can be done; that is, by emancipating the afterborn, leaving them, on due compensation, with their mothers, until their services are worth maintenance, and then putting them to industrious occupations, until a proper age for deportation . . . I have never yet been able to conceive any other practicable plan.

V. Minorities: Indians

Indians are primitive, but so were early Europeans
Notes on Virginia, Query 6

Before we condemn the Indians of this continent as wanting genius, we must consider that letters have not yet been introduced among them. Were we to compare them in their present state with the Europeans, north of the Alps, when the Roman arms and arts first crossed those mountains, the comparison would be unequal, because, at that time, those parts of Europe were swarming with numbers; because numbers produce emulation, and multiply the chances of improvement, and one improvement begets another. Yet I may safely ask, how many good poets, how many able mathematicians, how many great inventors in arts or sciences, had Europe, north of the Alps, then produced? And it was sixteen centuries after this before a Newton could be formed.

Indians have a right to freedom and happiness
Second Inaugural, March 4, 1805

The aboriginal inhabitants of these countries I have regarded with the commiseration their history inspires. Endowed with the faculties and the rights of men, breathing an ardent love of liberty and independence, and occupying a country which left them no desire but to be undisturbed, the stream of overflowing population from other regions directed itself on these shores; without power to divert, or habits to contend against, they have been overwhelmed by the current, or driven before it; now reduced within limits too narrow for the hunter's state, humanity enjoins us to teach them agriculture and the domestic arts; to encourage them to that industry which alone can enable them to maintain their place in existence, and to prepare them in time for that state of society, which to bodily comforts adds the improvement of the mind and morals. We have therefore liberally furnished them with the implements of husbandry and household use; we have placed among them instructors in the arts of first necessity; and they are covered with the ægis of the law against aggressors from among ourselves.

But the endeavors to enlighten them . . . have powerful obstacles to encounter; they are combated by the habits of their bodies, prejudice of their minds, ignorance, pride, and the influence of interested and crafty individuals among them, who feel themselves something in the present order of things, and fear to become nothing in any other. These persons inculcate a sanctimonious reverence for the customs of their ancestors; that whatsoever they did, must be done through all time; that reason is a false guide, and to advance under its counsel, in their physical, moral, or political condition, is perilous innovation; that their duty is to remain as their Creator made them, ignorance being safety, and knowledge full of danger; in short, my friends, among them is seen the action and counteraction of good sense and bigotry; they, too, have their anti-philosophers, who find an interest in keeping things in their present state, who dread reformation, and exert all their faculties to maintain the ascendancy of habit over the duty of improving our reason, and obeying its mandates.

Indians to live in peace and friendship
To the Wolf and People of the Mandar Nation, 1806

My friends and children, we are descended from the old nations which live beyond the great water, but we and our forefathers have been so long here that we seem like you to have grown out of this land. We consider ourselves no longer of the old nations beyond the great water, but as united in one family with our red brethren here. . . .

I have already told you that you and all the red men are my children, and I wish you to live in peace and friendship with one another as brethren of the same family ought to do. How much better is it for neighbors to help than to hurt one another; how much happier must it make them. If you will cease to make war on one another, if you will live in friendship with all mankind, you can employ all your time in providing food and clothing for yourselves and your families. Your men will not be destroyed in war, and your women and children will lie down to sleep in their cabins without fear of being surprised by their enemies and killed or carried away. Your numbers will be increased instead of diminishing, and you will live in plenty and quiet.

To receive governmental aid and instruction
To the Chiefs of the Shawanee Nation, 1897.

When the white people first came to this land, they were few, and you were many: now we are many, and you few; and why? Because, by cultivating the earth, we produce plenty to raise our children, while yours, during a part of every year, suffer for want of food, are forced to eat unwholesome things, are exposed to the weather in your hunting camps, get diseases and die. Hence it is that your numbers lessen.

You ask for instruction in our manner of living, for carpenters and blacksmiths. My children, you shall have them. We will do everything in our power to teach you to take care of your wives and children, that you may multiply and be strong. We are sincerely your friends and brothers, we are as unwilling to see your blood spilt in war, as our own. Therefore, we encourage you to live in peace with all nations, that your women and children may live without danger, and without fear. The greatest honor of a man is in doing good to his fellow men, not in destroying them.

Let the Indians settle down as cultivators
To Captain Hendrick, the Delawares, Mohiccons, and Munries, 1808 (?)

The picture which you have drawn, my son, of the increase of our numbers and the decrease of yours is just, the causes are very plain, and the remedy depends on yourselves alone. You have lived by hunting the deer and buffalo—all those have been driven westward; you have sold out on the seaboard and moved westwardly in pursuit of them. As they became scarce there, your food has failed you; you have been a part of every year without food, except the roots and other unwholesome things you could find in the forest. Scanty and unwholesome food produces disease and death among your children, and hence you have raised few and your numbers have decreased. Frequent wars, too, and the abuse of spirituous liquors, have assisted in lessening your numbers.

The whites, on the other hand, are in the habit of cultivating the earth, of raising stocks of cattle, hogs, and other domestic animals, in much greater numbers than they could kill of deer and buffalo. Having always a plenty of food and clothing they raise abundance of children, they double their numbers every twenty years, the new swarms are continually advancing upon the country like flocks of pigeons, and so they will continue to do. Now, my children, if we wanted to diminish our numbers, we would give up the culture of the earth, pursue the deer and buffalo, and be always at war; this would soon reduce us to be as few as you are, and if you wish to increase your numbers you must give up the deer and buffalo, live in peace, and cultivate the earth.

You see then, my children, that it depends on yourselves alone to become a numerous and great people. Let me entreat you, therefore, on the lands now given you to begin to give every man a farm; let him enclose it, cultivate it, build a warm house on it, and when he dies, let it belong to his wife and children after him. Nothing is so easy as to learn to cultivate the earth; all your women understand it, and to make it easier, we are always ready to teach you how to make plows, hoes, and necessary utensils. If the men will take the labor of the earth from the women they will learn to spin and weave and to clothe their families. In this way you will also raise many children, you will double your numbers every twenty years, and soon fill the land your friends have given you. . . . When once you have property, you will want laws and magistrates to protect your property and persons, and to punish those among you who commit crimes. You will find that our laws are good for this purpose; you will wish to live under them, you will unite yourselves with us, join in our great councils and form one people with us, and we shall all be Americans; you will mix with us by marriage, your blood will run in our veins, and will spread with us over this great island.

VI. IMMIGRATION

Doubts as to the wisdom of mass immigration
Notes on Virginia, Query 8

But are there no inconveniences to be thrown into the scale against the advantage expected from a multiplication of numbers by the importation of foreigners? It is for the happiness of those united in society to harmonize as much as possible in matters which they must of necessity transact together. Civil government being the sole object of forming societies, its administration must be conducted by common consent. Every species of government has its specific principles. Ours perhaps are more peculiar than those of any other in the universe. It is a composition of the freest principles of the English constitution, with others derived from natural right and natural reason. To these nothing can be more opposed than the maxims of absolute monarchies. Yet from such we are to expect the greatest number of emigrants. They will bring with them the principles of the governments they leave, imbibed in their early youth; or, if able to throw them off, it will be in exchange for an unbounded licentiousness, passing, as is usual, from one extreme to another. It would be a miracle were they to stop precisely at the point of temperate liberty. These principles, with their language, they will transmit to their children. In proportion to their numbers, they will share with us the legislation. They will infuse into it their spirit, warp and bias its directions, and render it a heterogeneous, incoherent, distracted mass . . .

Suppose twenty millions of republican Americans thrown all of a sudden into France, what would be the condition of that kingdom? If it would be more turbulent, less happy, less strong, we may believe that the addition of half a million of foreigners to our present numbers would produce a similar effect here.

If they come of themselves they are entitled to all the rights of citizenship; but I doubt the expediency of inviting them by extraordinary encouragements. I mean not that these doubts should be extended to the importation of useful artificers. The policy of that measure depends on very different considerations. Spare no expense in obtaining them. They will after a while go to the plow and the hoe; but, in the mean time, they will teach us something we do not know.

Grant asylum and citizenship to refugees
First Annual Message, December 8, 1801

And shall we refuse the unhappy fugitives from distress that hospitality which the savages of the wilderness extended to our fathers arriving in this land? Shall oppressed humanity find no asylum on this globe? The constitution, indeed, has wisely provided that, for admission to certain offices of important trust, a residence shall be required sufficient to develop character and design. But might not the general character and capabilities of a citizen be safely communicated to every one manifesting a bona fide purpose of embarking his life and fortunes permanently with us?

CHAPTER VI
RELIGION

CREDO

To Dr. Rush, 1800

THEY [the clergy] believe that any portion of power confided to me, will be exerted in opposition to their schemes. And they believe rightly: for I have sworn upon the altar of God, eternal hostility against every form of tyranny over the mind of man. But this is all they have to fear from me: and enough too in their opinion.

I. TOLERATION

Principles of toleration
Notes on Religion, October, 1776 (?)

How far does the duty of toleration extend?

1. No church is bound by the duty of toleration to retain within her bosom obstinate offenders against her law.

2. We have no right to prejudice another in his *civil* enjoiments because he is of another church. If any man err from

the right way it is his own misfortune, no injury to thee; nor therefore are thou to punish him in the things of this life because thou supposeth he will be miserable in that which is to come—on the contrary according to the spirit of the gospel, charity, bounty, liberality is due to him.

Each church being free, no one can have jurisdiction over another one, not even when the civil magistrate joins it. . . . Suppose for instance two churches, one of Arminians, another of Calvinists in Constantinople, has either any right over the other? Will it be said the orthodox one has? Every church is to itself orthodox; to *others* erroneous or heretical.

No man complains of his neighbor for ill management of his affairs, for an error in sowing his land, or marrying his daughter, for consuming his substance in taverns, pulling down building, etc ; in all these he has liberty: but if he does not frequent the church, or then conform to ceremonies, there is an immediate uproar.

The care of every man's soul belongs to himself. But what if he neglect the care of it? Well what if he neglect the care of his health or estate, which more nearly relate to the state. Will the magistrate make a law that he shall not be poor or sick? Laws provide against injury from others; but not from ourselves. God himself will not save men against their wills. . . .

If the magistrate command me to bring my commodity to a publick store house I bring it because he can indemnify me if he erred & I thereby lose it; but what indemnification can he give one for the kingdom of heaven?

I cannot give up my guidance to the magistrate, because he knows no more of the way to heaven than I do, & is less concerned to direct me right than I am to go right.

Arguments for religious freedom
Notes on Virginia, Query 17

The rights of conscience we never submitted, we could not submit. We are answerable for them to our God. The legitimate powers of government extend to such acts only as are injurious to others. But it does me no injury for my neighbor to say there are twenty gods, or no God. It neither picks my pocket nor breaks my leg. If it be said, his testimony in a court of justice cannot be relied on, reject it then, and be the stigma on him. Constraint may make him worse by making him a hypocrite, but it will never make him a truer man. It may fix him obstinately in his errors, but will not cure them.

Reason and free inquiry are the only effectual agents against error. Give a loose to them, they will support the true religion by bringing every false one to their tribunal, to the test of their investigation. They are the natural enemies of error only. Had not the Roman government permitted free inquiry, Christianity could never have been introduced. Had not free inquiry been indulged at the era of the reformation, the corruptions of Christianity could not have been purged away. If it be restrained now, the present corruptions will be protected, and new ones encouraged.

Was the government to prescribe to us our medicine and diet, our bodies would be in such keeping as our souls are now. Thus in France the emetic was once forbidden as a medicine, and the potato as an article of food. Government is just as infallible, too, when it fixes systems in physics. Galileo was sent to the Inquisition for affirming that the earth was a sphere; the government had declared it to be as flat as a trencher, and Galileo was obliged to abjure his error. This error, however, at length prevailed, the earth became a globe, and Descartes declared it was whirled round its axis by a vortex. The government in which he lived was wise enough to see that this was no question of civil jurisdiction, or we should all have been involved by authority in vortices. In fact, the vortices have been exploded, and the Newtonian principle of gravitation is now more firmly established, on the basis of reason, than it would be were the government to step in, and to make it an article of necessary faith. Reason and experiment have been indulged, and error has fled before them. It is error alone which needs the support of government. Truth can stand by itself.

Subject opinion to coercion: whom will you make your inquisitors? Fallible men; men governed by bad passions, by private as well as public reasons. And why subject it to coercion? To produce uniformity. But is uniformity of opinion desirable? No more than of face and stature. Introduce the bed of Procrustes then, and as there is danger that the large men may beat the small, make us all of a size, by lopping the former and stretching the latter. Difference of opinion is advantageous in religion. The several sects perform the office of a *censor morum* over such other.

Is uniformity attainable? Millions of innocent men, women, and children, since the introduction of Christianity have been burnt, tortured, fined, imprisoned; yet we have not advanced an inch towards uniformity. What has been the effect of coercion? To make one half the world fools, and the other half hypocrites. To support roguery and error all over the earth.

Let us reflect that it [the earth] is inhabited by a thousand millions of people. That these profess probably a thousand different systems of religion. That ours is but one of that thousand. That if there be but one right, and ours that one, we should wish to see the nine hundred and ninety-nine wandering sects gathered into the fold of truth. But against such a majority we cannot effect this by force. Reason and persuasion are the only practicable instruments. To make way for these, free inquiry must be indulged; and how can we wish others to indulge it while we refuse it ourselves.

But every State, says an inquisitor, has established some religion. No two, say I, have established the same. . . . Our sister States of Pennsylvania and New York, however, have long subsisted without any establishment at all. . . . They flourish infinitely. Religion is well supported; of various kinds, indeed, but all good enough. . . . They do not hang more malefactors than we do. They are not more disturbed with religious dissensions. On the contrary, their harmony is unparalleled, and can be ascribed to nothing but their unbounded tolerance. . . . They have made the happy discovery, that the way to silence religious disputes, is to take no notice of them. Let us too give this experiment fair play, and get rid, while we may, of those tyrannical laws.

It is true, we are as yet secured against them by the spirit of the times. I doubt whether the people of this country would suffer an execution for heresy, or a three years' imprisonment for not comprehending the mysteries of the Trinity. But is the spirit of the people an infallible, permanent reliance? Is it government? Is this the kind of protection we receive in return for the rights we give up? Besides, the spirit of the times may alter, will alter. Our rulers will become corrupt, our people careless. A single zealot may commence persecutor, and better men be his victims. It can never be too often repeated, that the time for fixing every essential right on a legal basis is while our rulers are honest, and ourselves united.

To Dufief, 1814

Are we to have a censor whose imprimatur shall say what

books may be sold, and what we may buy? And who is thus to dogmatize religious opinions for our citizens? Whose foot is to be the measure to which ours are all to be cut or stretched? Is a priest to be our inquisitor, or shall a layman, simple as ourselves, set up his reason as the rule for what we are to read, and what we must believe? It is an insult to our citizens to question whether they are rational beings or not, and blasphemy against religion to suppose it cannot stand the test of truth and reason. If M. de Becourt's book* be false in its facts, disprove them; if false in its reasoning, refute it. But, for God's sake, let us freely hear both sides, if we choose.

An Act for Establishing Religious Freedom Passed in the Assembly of Virginia, 1786

Well aware that Almighty God hath created the mind free;

that all attempts to influence it by temporal punishments or burdens, or by civil incapacitations, tend only to beget habits of hypocrisy and meanness, and are a departure from the plan of the Holy Author of our religion, who being Lord both of body and mind, yet chose not to propagate it by coercion on either, as was in his Almighty power to do;

that the impious presumption of legislators and rulers, civil as well as ecclesiastical, who, being themselves but fallible and uninspired men have assumed dominion over the faith of others, setting up their own opinions and modes of thinking as the only true and infallible, and as such endeavoring to impose them on others, hath established and maintained false religions over the greatest part of the world, and through all time;

that to compel a man to furnish contributions of money for the propagation of opinions which he disbelieves, is sinful and tyrannical;

that even the forcing him to support this or that teacher of his own religious persuasion, is depriving him of the comfortable liberty of giving his contributions to the particular pastor whose morals he would make his pattern, and whose powers he feels most persuasive to righteousness, and is withdrawing from the ministry those temporal rewards, which proceeding from an approbation of their personal conduct, are an additional incitement to earnest and unremitting labors for the instruction of mankind;

* Sur la Création du Monde, un Système d'Organisation Primitive.

that our civil rights have no dependence on our religious opinions, more than our opinions in physics or geometry;

that, therefore, the proscribing of any citizen as unworthy of the public confidence by laying upon him an incapacity of being called to the offices of trust and emolument, unless he profess or renounce this or that religious opinion, is depriving him injuriously of those privileges and advantages to which in common with his fellow citizens he has a natural right;

that it tends also to corrupt the principles of that very religion it is meant to encourage, by bribing, with a monopoly of worldly honors and emoluments, those who will externally profess and conform to it;

that though indeed these are criminal who do not withstand such temptation, yet neither are those innocent who lay the bait in their way;

that to suffer the civil magistrate to intrude his powers into the field of opinion and to restrain the profession or propagation of principles, on the supposition of their ill tendency, is a dangerous fallacy, which at once destroys all religious liberty, because he being of course judge of that tendency, will make his opinions the rule of judgment, and approve or condemn the sentiments of others only as they shall square with or differ from his own;

that it is time enough for the rightful purposes of civil government, for its officers to interfere when principles break out into overt acts against peace and good order;

and finally, that truth is great and will prevail if left to herself, that she is the proper and sufficient antagonist to error, and has nothing to fear from the conflict, unless by human interposition disarmed of her natural weapons, free argument and debate, errors ceasing to be dangerous when it is permitted freely to contradict them.

Be it therefore enacted by the General Assembly,

That no man shall be compelled to frequent or support any religious worship, place or ministry whatsoever, nor shall be enforced, restrained, molested, or burthened in his body or goods, nor shall otherwise suffer on account of his religious opinions or belief; but that all men shall be free to profess, and by argument to maintain, their opinions in matters of religion, and that the same shall in nowise diminish, enlarge, or affect their civil capacities.

And though we well know this Assembly, elected by the people for the ordinary purposes of legislation only, have no power to restrain the acts of succeeding assemblies, constituted with the powers equal to our own, and that therefore to declare this act irrevocable, would be of no effect in law, yet we are free to declare, and do declare, that the rights hereby asserted are of the natural rights of mankind, and that if any act shall be hereafter passed to repeal the present or to narrow its operation, such act will be an infringement of natural right.

European admiration for the Act of Religious Freedom
To Wythe, 1786

Our act for freedom of religion is extremely applauded. The ambassadors and ministers of the several nations of Europe, resident at this court, have asked of me copies of it, to send to their sovereigns, and it is inserted at full length in several books now in the press; among others, in the new Encyclopédie. I think it will produce considerable good even in these countries, where ignorance, superstition, poverty, and oppression of body and mind, in every form, are so firmly settled on the mass of the people, that their redemption from them can never be hoped. If all the sovereigns of Europe were to set themselves to work, to emancipate the minds of their subjects from their present ignorance and prejudices, and that, as zealously as they now endeavor the contrary, a thousand years would not place them on that high ground, on which our common people are now setting out. Ours could not have been so fairly placed under the control of the common sense of the people, had they not been separated from their parent stock, and kept from contamination, either from them, or the other people of the old world, by the intervention of so wide an ocean.

To Madison, 1786

The Virginia act for religious freedom has been received with infinite approbation in Europe, and propagated with enthusiasm. I do not mean by the governments, but by the individuals who compose them. It has been translated into French and Italian, has been sent to most of the courts of Europe, and has been the best evidence of the falsehood of those reports which stated us to be in anarchy. It is inserted in the new Encyclopédie, and is appearing in most of the publications respecting America. In fact, it is comfortable to see the standard of reason at length erected, after so many ages, during which the human mind has been held in vassalage by kings, priests, and nobles; and it is honorable for us, to have produced the first legislature who had the courage to declare, that the reason of man may be trusted with the formation of his own opinions.

Freedom of conscience
To Edward Dowse, 1803

I never will, by any word or act, bow to the shrine of intolerance, or admit a right of inquiry into the religious opinions of others. On the contrary, we are bound, you, I, and every one, to make common cause, even with error itself, to maintain the common right of freedom of conscience. We ought with one heart and one hand to hew down the daring and dangerous efforts of those who would seduce the public opinion to substitute itself into . . . tyranny over religious faith.

Separation of Church and State: a "loathsome combination"
To Attorney-General Lincoln, 1802

Averse to receive addresses, yet unable to prevent them, I have generally endeavored to turn them to some account, by making them the occasion, by way of answer, of sowing useful truths and principles among the people, which might germinate and become rooted among their political tenets. The Baptist address, now enclosed, admits of a condemnation of the alliance between Church and State, under the authority of the constitution. It furnishes an occasion, too, which I have long wished to find, of saying why I do not proclaim fasting and thanksgiving, as my predecessors did. . . . I know it will give great offense to the New England clergy; but the advocate of religious freedom is to expect neither peace nor forgiveness from them.

To Rev. Samuel Miller, 1808

I consider the government of the United States as interdicted by the Constitution from intermeddling with religious institutions, their doctrines, discipline or exercises. . . . I do not believe it is for the interest of religion to invite the civil magistrate to direct its exercises, its discipline, or its doctrines. . . . Every one must act according to the dictates of his own reason, and mine tells me that civil powers alone have been given to the President of the United States and no authority to direct the religious exercises of his constituents.

To J. Fishback, 1809

Reading, reflection and time have convinced me that the interests of society require the observation of those moral precepts only in which all religions agree (for all forbid us to murder, steal, plunder, or bear false witness) and that we should not intermeddle with the particular dogmas in which all religions differ, and which are totally unconnected with morality. In all of them we see good men, and as many in one as another. The varieties in structure and action of the human mind as in those of the body, are the work of our Creator, against which it cannot be a religious duty to erect the standard of uniformity. The practice of morality being necessary for the well-being of society, he has taken care to impress its precepts so indelibly on our hearts that they shall not be effaced by the subtleties of our brain. We all agree in the obligation of the moral precepts of Jesus.

To C. Clay, 1815

Government, as well as religion, has furnished its schisms, its persecutions, and its devices for fattening idleness on the earnings of the people. It has its hierarchy of emperors, kings, princes and nobles, as that has of popes, cardinals, archbishops, bishops and priests. In short cannibals are not to be found in the wilds of America only, but are reveling on the blood of every living people. Turning, then, from this loathsome combination of Church and State, and weeping over the follies of our fellow men who yield themselves the willing dupes and drudges of these mountebanks, I consider reformation and redress as desperate, and abandon them to the Quixotism of more enthusiastic minds.

Toleration for Jews
To De la Motte, 1820

It excites in [me] the gratifying reflection that [my] own country has been the first to prove to the world two truths, the most salutary to human society, that man can govern himself, and that religious freedom is the most effectual anodyne against religious dissension. . . . [I am] happy in the restoration, of the Jews particularly, to their social rights, and hope they will be seen taking their seats on the benches of science, as preparatory to their doing the same at the board of government.

To Jos. Marx, 1820

[I have] ever felt regret at seeing a sect, the parent and basis of all those of Christendom, singled out by all of them for a persecution and oppression which proved they have profited nothing from the benevolent doctrines of him whom they profess to make the model of their principle and practice.

II. Criticism of Christianity

Perversion of pure morality
To S. Kercheval, 1810

But a short time elapsed after the death of the great reformer of the Jewish religion, before his principles were departed from by those who professed to be his special servants, and perverted into an engine for enslaving mankind, and aggrandizing their oppressors in Church and State: that the purest system of morals ever before preached to man has been adulterated and sophisticated by artificial constructions, into a mere contrivance to filch wealth and power to themselves: that rational men, not being able to swallow their impious heresies, in order to force them down their throats, they raise the hue and cry of infidelity, while themselves are the greatest obstacles to the advancement of the real doctrines of Jesus, and do, in fact, constitute the real Anti-Christ.

Platonic mysticism
To Adams, 1813

It is too late in the day for men of sincerity to pretend they believe in the Platonic mysticisms that three are one, and one is three; and yet that the one is not three, and the three are not one. . . . But this constitutes the craft, the power and the profit of the priests. Sweep away their gossamer fabrics of factitious religion, and they would catch no more flies. We should all then, like the Quakers, live without an order of priests, moralize for ourselves, follow the oracle of conscience, and say nothing about what no man can understand, nor therefore believe.

To Dr. Waterhouse, 1815

The priests have so disfigured the simple religion of Jesus that no one who reads the sophistications they have engrafted on it, from the jargon of Plato, of Aristotle and other mystics, would conceive these could have been fathered on the sublime preacher of the Sermon on the Mount. Yet, knowing the importance of names, they have assumed that of Christians, while they are mere Platonists, or anything rather than disciples of Jesus.

Unintelligible dogmas
To Carey, 1816: N. Y. Pub. Lib., MS, IV, 409

On the dogmas of religion, as distinguished from moral principles, all mankind, from the beginning of the world to this day, have been quarreling, fighting, burning and torturing one another, for abstractions unintelligible to themselves and to all others, and absolutely beyond the comprehension of the human mind. Were I to enter on that arena, I should only add an unit to the number of Bedlamites.

Obscurantist charlatanism
To Van der Kemp, 1816

Altho' I rarely waste time in reading on theological subjects, as mangled by our Pseudo-Christians, yet I can readily suppose Basanistos may be amusing. Ridicule is the only weapon which can be used against unintelligible propositions. Ideas must be distinct before reason can act upon them; and no man ever had a distinct idea of the trinity. It is mere Abracadabra of the mountebanks calling themselves the priests of Jesus. If it could be understood it would not answer their purpose. Their security is in their faculty of shedding darkness, like the scuttle-fish, thro' the element in which they move, and making it impenetrable to the eye of a pursuing enemy, and there they will skulk.

Education must dissipate obscurantism
To Van der Kemp, 1820

The genuine and simple religion of Jesus will one day be restored: such as it was preached and practised by himself. Very soon after his death it became muffled up in mysteries, and has been ever since kept in concealment from the vulgar eye. To penetrate and dissipate these clouds of darkness, the general mind must be strengthened by education.

III. INDIVIDUAL SECTS

Quakers
To S. Kercheval, 1810

The theory of American Quakerism is a very obvious one. The mother society is in England. Its members are English by birth and residence, devoted to their own country as good citizens ought to be. The Quakers of these States are colonies or filiations from the mother society, to whom that society sends its yearly lessons. On these, the filiated societies model their opinions, their conduct, their passions and attachments. A Quaker is essentially an Englishman, in whatever part of the earth he is born or lives. . . . The Quakers here have taken side against their own government, not on their *profession* of peace, for they saw that peace was our object also; but from devotion to the views of the mother society. In 1797-98, when an administration sought war with France, the Quakers were the most clamorous for war. Their principle of peace, as a secondary one, yielded to the primary one of adherence to the Friends in England, and what was patriotism in the original, became treason in the copy. . . . I apply this to the Friends in general, not universally. I know individuals among them as good patriots as we have.

To Wm. Canby, 1813

An eloquent [Quaker] preacher . . . is said to have exclaimed aloud to his congregation, that he did not believe there was a Quaker, Presbyterian, Methodist or Baptist in heaven. . . . He added, that in heaven God knew no distinctions, but considered all good men as his children, and as brethren of the same family. I believe, with the Quaker preacher, that he who steadily observes those moral precepts in which all religions concur, will never be questioned at the gates of heaven, as to the dogmas in which they all differ. . . . Of all the systems of morality, ancient or modern, which have come under my observation, none appear to me so pure as that of Jesus.

Presbyterians
To W. Short, 1820

The Presbyterian clergy are loudest; the most intolerant of all sects, the most tyrannical and ambitious; ready at the word of the lawgiver, if such a word could be now obtained, to put the torch to the pile, and to rekindle in this virgin hemisphere, the flames in which their oracle Calvin consumed the poor Servetus, because he could not find in his Euclid the proposition which has demonstrated that three are one and one is three, nor subscribe to that of Calvin, that magistrates have a right to exterminate all heretics to Calvinistic Creed. They pant to reëstablish, *by law,* that holy inquisition, which they can now only infuse into *public opinion*. We have most unwisely committed to the hierophants of our particular superstition, the direction of public opinion, that lord of the universe. We have given them stated and privileged days to collect and catechise us, opportunities of delivering their oracles to the people in mass, and of molding their minds as wax in the hollow of their hands. But in despite of their fulminations against endeavors to enlighten the general mind, to improve the reason of the people, and to encourage them in the use of it, the liberality of this State will support this institution [University of Virginia], and give fair play to the cultivation of reason.

Calvinists
To Adams, 1823

I can never join Calvin in addressing *his God*. He was indeed an atheist, which I can never be; or rather his religion was dæmonism. If ever a man worshiped a false God, he did. The being described in his five points, is not the God whom you and I acknowledge and adore, the creator and benevolent governor of the world, but a dæmon of malignant spirit. It would be more pardonable to believe in no God at all, than to blaspheme him by the atrocious attributes of Calvin. Indeed, I think that every Christian sect gives a great handle to atheism by their general dogma, that, without a revelation, there would not be sufficient proof of the being of a God. Now one-sixth of mankind only are supposed to be Christians; the other five-sixths then, who do not believe in the Jewish and Christian revelation, are without a knowledge of the existence of a God!

IV. CHARACTER OF JESUS

His sublime morality
To W. Short, 1820

It is not to be understood that I am with him [Jesus] in all his doctrines. I am a Materialist; he takes the side of Spiritualism; he preaches the efficacy of repentance towards forgiveness of sin; I require a counterpoise of good works to redeem it, etc. It is the innocence of his character, the purity and sublimity of his moral precepts, the eloquences of his inculcations, the beauty of the apologues in which he conveys them, that I so much admire; sometimes, indeed, needing indulgence to eastern hyperbolism. My eulogies, too, may be founded on a postulate which all may not be ready to grant. Among the sayings and discourses imputed to him by his biographers, I find many passages of fine imagination, correct morality, and of the most lovely benevolence; and others, again, of so much ignorance, so much absurdity, so much untruth, charlatanism and imposture, as to pronounce it impossible that such contradictions should have proceeded from the same being. I separate, therefore, the gold from the dross; restore to him the former, and leave the latter to the stupidity of some, and roguery of others of his disciples. Of this band of dupes and impostors, Paul was the great Coryphæus, and first corruptor of the doctrines of Jesus.

His mind and faith
To W. Short, 1820

The office of reformer of the superstitions of a nation, is ever dangerous. Jesus had to walk on the perilous confines of reason and religion; and a step to the right or left might place him within the grasp of the priests of the superstition, a blood-thirsty race, as cruel and remorseless as the being whom they represented as the family God of Abraham, of Isaac and of Jacob, and the local God of Israel. They were constantly laying snares, too, to entangle him in the web of the law. He was justifiable, therefore, in avoiding these by evasions, by sophisms, by misconstructions and misapplications of scraps of the prophets, and in defending himself with these their own weapons, as sufficient, *ad homines,* at least. That Jesus did not mean to impose himself on mankind as the son of God, physically speaking, I have been convinced by the writings of men more learned than myself in that lore. But that he might conscientiously believe himself inspired from above, is very possible. The whole religion of the Jew, inculcated in him from his infancy, was founded in the belief of divine inspiration. The fumes of the most disordered imaginations were recorded in their religious code, as special communications of the Deity. . . . Elevated by the enthusiasm of a warm and pure heart, conscious of the high strains of an eloquence which had not been taught him, he might readily mistake the coruscations of his own fine genius for inspirations of an higher order. This belief carried, therefore, no more personal imputation, than the belief of Socrates, that himself was under the care and admonitions of a guardian Dæmon.

V. Personal Faith

". . . *thinking for myself*"
To Hopkinson, 1789

I am not a federalist, because I never submitted the whole system of my opinions to the creed of any party of men whatever, in religion, in philosophy, in politics or in anything else, where I was capable of thinking for myself. Such an addiction, is the last degradation of a free and moral agent. If I could not go to heaven but with a party, I would not go there at all.

"*I am a real Christian*"
To C. Thompson, 1816

I am a *real Christian*, that is to say, a disciple of the doctrines of Jesus, very different from the Platonists, who call *me* infidel and *themselves* Christians and preachers of the gospel, while they draw all their characteristic dogmas from what its author never said nor saw. They have compounded from the heathen mysteries a system beyond the comprehension of man, of which the great reformer of the vicious ethics of deism of the Jews, were he to return on earth, would not recognize one feature.

"*Not afraid of the priests*"
To H. G. Spafford, 1816

I am not afraid of the priests. They have tried upon me all their various batteries, of pious whining, hypocritical canting, lying and slandering, without being able to give me one moment of pain. I have contemplated their order from the Magi of the East to the Saints of the West, and I have found no difference of character, but of more or less caution, in proportion to their information or ignorance of those on whom their interested duperies were to be plaid off. Their sway in New England is indeed formidable. No mind beyond mediocrity dares there to develop itself.

Do good, eschew evil
To E. Styles, 1819

I am not [a Calvinist]. I am of a sect by myself, as far as I know. I am not a Jew, and therefore do not adopt their theology, which supposes the God of infinite justice to punish the sins of the fathers upon their children, unto the third and fourth generation; and the benevolent and sublime reformer of that religion has told us only that God is good and perfect, but has not defined him. I am, therefore, of his theology, believing that we have neither words nor ideas adequate to that definition. And if we could all, after this example, leave the subject as undefinable, we should all be of one sect, doers of good, and eschewers of evil. No doctrines of his lead to schism. It is the speculations of crazy theologists which have made a Babel of a religion the most moral and sublime ever preached to man, and calculated to heal, and not to create differences. These religious animosities I impute to those who call themselves his ministers, and who engraft their casuistries on the stock of his simple precepts. I am sometimes more angry with them than is authorized by the blessed charities which he preaches.

CHAPTER VII

FOREIGN AFFAIRS

I. WAR

Man is a warlike animal
   To Madison, 1797

IN THE whole animal kingdom I recollect no family but man, steadily and systematically employed in the destruction of itself. Nor does what is called civilization produce any other effect, than to teach him to pursue the principle of the *bellum omnium in omnia* on a greater scale, and instead of the little contest between tribe and tribe, to comprehend all the quarters of the earth in the same work of destruction. If to this we add, that as to other animals, the lions and tigers are mere lambs compared with man as a destroyer, we must conclude that nature has been able to find in man alone a sufficient barrier against the too great multiplication of other animals and of man himself, an equilibrating power against the fecundity of generation.

Man seems to be a natural killer
   To Adams, 1822

To turn to the news of the day, it seems that the Cannibals of Europe are going to eating one another again. A war between Russia and Turkey is like the battle of the kite and snake. Whichever destroys the other, leaves a destroyer the less for the world. This pugnacious humor of mankind seems to be the law of his nature, one of the obstacles to too great multiplication provided in the mechanism of the Universe. The cocks of the henyard kill one another up. Bears, bulls, rams, do the same. And the horse, in his wild state, kills all the young males, until worn down with age and war, some vigorous youth kills him, and takes to himself the Harem of females. I hope we shall prove how much happier for man the Quaker policy is, and that the life of the feeder, is better than that of the fighter; and it is some consolation that the desolation by these maniacs of one part of the earth is the means of improving it in other parts. Let the latter be our office, and let us milk the cow, while the Russian holds her by the horns, and the Turk by the tail.

European lions and tigers
  To Dr. Benjamin Rush, 1803

Tremendous times in Europe! How mighty this battle of lions and tigers! With what sensations should the common herd of cattle look on it? With no partialities, certainly. If they can so far worry one another as to destroy their power for tyrannizing, the one over the earth, the other the waters, the world may perhaps enjoy peace, till they recruit again.

Loathing for European savagery
  To Colonel Duane, 1813

It is true that I am tired of practical politics, and happier while reading the history of ancient than of modern times. The total banishment of all moral principle from the code which governs the intercourse of nations, the melancholy reflection that after the mean, wicked and cowardly cunning of the cabinets of the age of Machiavel had given place to the integrity and good faith which dignified the succeeding one of a Chatham and Turgot, that this is to be swept away again by the daring profligacy and avowed destitution of all moral principle . . . , sickens my soul unto death. I turn from the contemplation with loathing, and take refuge in the histories of other times, where, if they also furnished their Tarquins, their Catalines and Caligulas, their stories are handed to us under the brand of a Livy, a Sallust and a Tacitus, and we are comforted with the reflection that the condemnation of all succeeding generations has confirmed the censures of the historian, and consigned their memories to everlasting infamy, a solace we cannot have with the Georges and Napoleons but by anticipation.

Barbarism over Europe
    To the Ketocton Baptist Association, 1808

The moral principles and conventional usages which have heretofore been the bond of civilized nations . . . have now given way to force, the law of Barbarians, and the nineteenth century dawns with the Vandalism of the fifth.

The rule of violence in international affairs
    To—(?), 1813: N. Y. Pub. Lib., MS, IV, 191-92

Our lot happens to have been cast in an age when two of the most powerful nations of the world, abusing their force and to whom circumstances have given a temporary superiority over others, the one by land, the other by sea, throwing off all the bonds [and] restraints of morality and all regard to pride of national character, forgetting the mutability of fortune and the inevitable doom which the laws of nature pronounce against departures from justice, individual or national—have dared to treat her reclamations with derision and to substitute force instead of reason as the umpire of nations, degrading themselves thus from the character of lawful societies into lawless bands of robbers and pirates, they are ravaging [and] abusing their brief ascendancy by desolating the world with blood and rapine. Against such banditti, war had become preferable [and] less ruinous than peace, for their peace was a war on one side only.

Rapacity of both England and France
    To J. Maury, 1812

We consider the overwhelming power of England on the ocean, and of France on the land, as destructive of the prosperity and happiness of the world, and wish both to be reduced only to the necessity of observing moral duties. We believe no more in Bonaparte's fighting merely for the liberty of the seas, than in Great Britain's fighting for the liberties of mankind. The object of both is the same, to draw to themselves the power, the wealth and the resources of other nations.

Hope for peace and liberty
    To Adams, 1821

I shall not die without a hope that light and liberty are on steady advance. We have seen, indeed, once within the records of history, a complete eclipse of the human mind continuing for centuries. And this, too, by swarms of the same northern barbarians, conquering and taking possession of the countries and governments of the civilized world. Should this be again attempted, should the same northern hordes, allured again by the corn, wine, and oil of the south, be able to settle their swarms in the countries of their growth, the art of printing alone, and the vast dissemination of books, will maintain the mind where it is, and raise the conquering ruffians to the level of the conquered, instead of degrading these to that of their conquerors. And even should the cloud of barbarism and despotism again obscure the science and liberties of Europe, this country remains to preserve and restore light and liberty to them. In short, the flames kindled on the 4th of July, 1776, have spread over too much of the globe to be extinguished by the feeble engines of despotism; on the contrary, they will consume these engines and all who work them.

II. No Entanglement

Abandon the ocean and escape war
  Notes on Virginia, Query 22

Never was so much false arithmetic employed on any subject, as that which has been employed to persuade nations that it is their interest to go to war. Were the money which it has cost to gain, at the close of a long war, a little town, or a little territory, the right to cut wood here, or to catch fish there, expended in improving what they already possess, in making roads, opening rivers, building ports, improving the arts, and finding employment for their idle poor, it would render them much stronger, much wealthier and happier. This I hope will be our wisdom.

And, perhaps, to remove as much as possible the occasions of making war, it might be better for us to abandon the ocean altogether, that being the element whereon we shall be principally exposed to jostle with other nations; to leave to others to bring what we shall want, and to carry what we can spare. This would make us invulnerable to Europe, by offering none of our property to their prize, and would turn all our citizens to the cultivation of the earth; and, I repeat it again, cultivators of the earth are the most virtuous and independent citizens. It might be time enough to seek employment for them at sea, when the land no longer offers it. But the actual habits of our countrymen attach them to commerce. They will exercise it for themselves. Wars then must sometimes be our lot; and all the wise can do, will be to avoid that half of them which would be produced by our own follies and our own acts of injustice; and to make for the other half the best preparations we can.

To Pendleton, 1799

What a glorious exchange would it be could we persuade our navigating fellow citizens to embark their capital in the internal commerce of our country, exclude foreigners from that and let them take the carrying trade in exchange: abolish the diplomatic establishments and never suffer an armed vessel of any nation to enter our ports.

Sever relations with an international aggressor
To T. Coxe, 1794

I love peace, and I am anxious that we should give the world still another useful lesson, by showing to them other modes of punishing injuries than by war, which is as much a punishment to the punisher as to the sufferer. I love, therefore . . . [the] proposition of cutting off all communications with the nation [England] which has conducted itself so atrociously. This, you will say, may bring on war. If it does, we will meet it like men; but it may not bring on war, and then the experiment will have been a happy one.

Plan for neutrality
To E. Rutledge, 1797

What the neutral nations think of us now, I know not; but we are low indeed with the belligerents. Their kicks and cuffs prove their contempt. If we weather the present storm, I hope we shall avail ourselves of the calm of peace, to place our foreign connections under a new and different arrangement. We must make the interest of every nation stand surety for their justice, and their own loss to follow injury to us, as effect follows its cause. As to everything except commerce, we ought to divorce ourselves from them all. But this system would require time, temper, wisdom, and occasional sacrifice of interest; and how far all of these will be ours, our children may see, but we shall not.

Horror of European entanglements
To Wm. Short, 1801

We have a perfect horror at everything like connecting ourselves with the politics of Europe. It would indeed be advantageous to us to have neutral rights established on a broad ground; but no dependence can be placed in any European coalition for that. They have so many other bye-interests of greater weight, that some one or other will always be bought off. To be entangled with them would be a much greater evil than a temporary acquiescence in the false principles which have prevailed.

Third Annual Message, October 17, 1803

Separated by a wide ocean from the nations of Europe, and from the political interests which entangle them together, with productions and wants which render our commerce and friendship useful to them and theirs to us, it cannot be the interest of any to assail us, nor ours to disturb them. We should be most unwise, indeed, were we to cast away the singular blessings of the position in which nature has placed us, the opportunity she has endowed us with of pursuing, at a distance from foreign contentions, the paths of industry, peace, and happiness; of cultivating general friendship, and of bringing collisions of interest to the umpirage of reason rather than of force. How desirable then must it be, in a government like ours, to see its citizens adopt individually the views, the interests, and the conduct which their country should pursue, divesting themselves of those passions and partialities which tend to lessen useful friendships, and to embarrass and embroil us in the calamitous scenes of Europe.

Maritime neutrality
Third Annual Message, October 17, 1803

In the course of this conflict, let it be our endeavor, as it is our interest and desire, to cultivate the friendship of the belligerent nations by every act of justice and of incessant kindness; to receive their armed vessels with hospitality from the distresses of the sea, but to administer the means of annoyance to none; to establish in our harbors such a police as may maintain law and order; to restrain our citizens from embarking individually in a war in which their country takes no part; to punish severely those persons, citizen or alien, who shall usurp the cover of our flag for vessels not entitled to it, infecting thereby with suspicion those of real Americans, and committing us into controversies for the redress of wrongs not our own; to exact from every nation the observance, toward our vessels and citizens, of those principles and practices of a just nation, and maintain that of an independent one, preferring every consequence to insult and habitual wrong.

Isolation
To Tammany Society, 1808

There can be no question, in a mind truly American, whether it is best to send our citizens and property into certain captivity, and then wage war for their recovery, or to keep them at home, and to turn seriously to that policy which plants the manufacturer and the husbandman side by side, and establishes at the door of every one that exchange of mutual labors and comforts, which we have hitherto sought in distant regions, and under perpetual risk of broils with them.

To Bloodgood and Hammond, 1809

A world in arms and trampling on all those moral principles which have heretofore been deemed sacred in the intercourse between nations, could not suffer us to remain insensible of all agitation. During such a course of lawless violence, it was certainly wise to withdraw ourselves from all intercourse with the belligerent nations, to avoid the desolating calamities inseparable from war, its pernicious effects on manners and morals, and the dangers it threatened to free governments; and to cultivate our own resources until our natural and progressive growth should leave us nothing to fear from foreign enterprise.

Nature of American pacifism
To the Earl of Buchan, 1803

[I] bless the Almighty Being, who, in gathering together the waters under the heavens into one place, divided the dry land of your hemisphere from the dry lands of ours, and said, at least be there peace. I hope that peace and amity with all nations will long be the character of our land, and that its prosperity under the Charter will react on the mind of Europe, and profit her by the example. My hope of preserving peace for our country is not founded in the greater principles of non-resistance under every wrong, but in the belief that a just and friendly conduct on our part will procure justice and friendship from others.

Light of American freedom must be preserved for humanity
To the Citizens of Washington, March 4, 1809

The station which we occupy among the nations of the earth is honorable, but awful. Trusted with the destinies of this solitary republic of the world, the only monument of human rights, and the sole depository of the sacred fire of freedom and self-government, from hence it is to be lighted up in other regions of the earth, if other regions of the earth shall ever become susceptible of its benign influence. All mankind ought then, with us, to rejoice in its prosperous, and sympathize in its adverse fortunes, as involving everything dear to man. And to what sacrifices of interest, or convenience, ought not these considerations to animate us? To what compromises of opinion and inclination, to maintain harmony and union among ourselves, and to preserve from all danger this hallowed ark of human hope and happiness.

To the New York State Legislature, 1809

Sole depositories of the remains of human liberty, our duty to ourselves, to posterity, and to mankind, call on us by every motive which is sacred or honorable, to watch over the safety of our beloved country during the troubles which agitate and convulse the residue of the world, and to sacrifice to that all personal and local considerations. While the boasted energies of monarchy have yielded to easy conquest . . . , should our fabric of freedom suffer no more than the slight agitations we have experienced, it will be an useful lesson to the friends as well as the enemies of self-government.

Compared to Europe, America is paradise
To Dr. Jones, 1810

Our difficulties are indeed great, if we consider ourselves alone. But when viewed in comparison to those of Europe, they are the joys of Paradise. In the eternal revolution of ages, the destinies have placed our portion of existence amidst such scenes of tumult and outrage, as no other period, within our knowledge, has presented. Every government but one on the continent of Europe, demolished, a conqueror roaming over the earth with havoc and destruction, a pirate spreading misery and ruin over the face of the ocean. Indeed . . . , ours is a bed of roses. And the system of government which shall keep us afloat amidst the wreck of the world, will be immortalized in history. We have, to be sure, our petty squabbles and heart burnings, and we have something of the blue devils at times, as to these raw heads and bloody bones who are eating up other nations. But happily for us, the Mammoth cannot swim, nor the Leviathan move on dry land; and if we will keep out of their way, they cannot get at us. If, indeed, we choose to place ourselves within the scope of their tether, a gripe of the paw, or flounce of the tail, may be our fortune.

To Adams, 1812

And I do believe we shall continue to growl, to multiply and prosper until we exhibit an association, powerful, wise and happy, beyond what has yet been seen by men. As for France and England, with all their preeminence in science, the one is a den of robbers, and the other of pirates. And if science produces no better fruits than tyranny, murder, rapine and destitution of national morality, I would rather wish our country to be ignorant, honest and estimable, as our neighboring savages are.

To Ticknor, 1816: N. Y. Pub. Lib., MS, IV, 338

I expect that Europe will again be in a state of general conflagration. What a divine contrast is the calm of our condition to the Volcanic state of that. How do our little party bickerings and squabbles shrink to nothing compared with the fire and sword and havoc of that Arena of gladiators.

Advantages of neutrality
To Eppes, 1811

I am so far . . . from believing that our reputation will be tarnished by our not having mixed in the mad contests of the rest of the world that, setting aside the ravings of pepper-pot politicians, of whom there are enough in every age and country, I believe it will place us high in the scale of wisdom, to have preserved our country tranquil and prosperous during a contest which prostrated the honor, power, independence, laws and property of every country on the other side of the Atlantic. Which of them have better preserved their honor? Has Spain, has Portugal, Italy, Switzerland, Holland, Prussia, Austria, the other German powers, Sweden, Denmark, or even Russia? And would we accept of the infamy of France or England in exchange for our honest reputation, or of the result of their enormities, despotism to the one, and bankruptcy and prostration to the other, in exchange for the prosperity, the freedom and independence which we have preserved safely through the wreck?

To save our democracy, all Americans must unite
To Colonel Wm. Duane, 1811

During the *bellum omnium in omnia* of Europe, [our country] will require the union of all its friends to resist its enemies within and without. . . . The last hope of human liberty in this world rests on us. We ought, for so dear a state, to sacrifice every attachment and every enmity. Leave the

President free to choose his own coadjutors, to pursue his own measures, and support him and them, even if we think we are wiser than they, honester than they are, or possessing more enlarged information of the state of things. If we move in mass, be it ever so circuitously, we shall attain our object; but if we break into squads, every one pursuing the path he thinks most direct, we become an easy conquest to those who can now barely hold us in check.

I repeat again, that we ought not to schismatize on either men or measures. Principles alone can justify that. If we find our government in all its branches rushing headlong, like our predecessors, into the arms of monarchy, if we find them violating our dearest rights, the trial by jury, the freedom of the press, the freedom of opinion, civil or religious, or opening on our peace of mind or personal safety the sluices of terrorism, if we see them raising standing armies, when the absence of all other danger points to these as the sole objects on which they are to be employed, then indeed let us withdraw and call the nation to its tents. But while our functionaries are wise, and honest, and vigilant, let us move compactly under their guidance, and we have nothing to fear. Things may here and there go a little wrong. It is not in their power to prevent it. But all will be right in the end, though not perhaps by the shortest means.

Peace must be our principle—and hope
  To Kosciuszko, 1811

But when we see two antagonists contending *ad internecionem,* so eager for mutual destruction as to disregard all means, to deal their blows in every direction regardless on whom they may fall, prudent bystanders, whom some of them may wound, instead of thinking it cause to join in the maniac contest, get out of the way as well as they can, and leave the cannibals to mutual ravin. It would have been perfect Quixotism in us to have encountered these Bedlamites, to have undertaken the redress of all wrongs against a world avowedly rejecting all regard to right. We have, therefore, remained in peace, suffering frequent injuries, but, on the whole, multiplying, improving, prospering beyond all example. It is evident to all, that in spite of great losses much greater gains have ensued. When these gladiators shall have worried each other into ruin or reason, instead of lying among the dead on the bloody arena, we shall have acquired a growth and strength which will place us *hors d'insulte*. Peace then has been our principle, peace is our interest, and peace has saved the world this only plant of free and rational government now existing on it.

Fundamental maxim: No entanglement
To President Monroe, 1823

Our first and fundamental maxim should be, never to entangle ourselves in the broils of Europe. Our second, never to suffer Europe to intermeddle with cis-Atlantic affairs. America, North and South, has a set of interests distinct from those of Europe, and peculiarly her own. She should therefore have a system of her own, separate and apart from that of Europe. While the last is laboring to become the domicil of despotism, our endeavor should surely be, to make our hemisphere that of freedom.

To President Monroe, 1823

I have ever deemed it fundamental for the United States, never to take active part in the quarrels of Europe. Their political interests are entirely distinct from ours. Their mutual jealousies, their balance of power, their complicated alliances, their forms and principles of government, are all foreign to us. They are nations of eternal war. All their energies are expended in the destruction of the labor, property and lives of their people. On our part, never had a people so favorable a chance of trying the opposite system, of peace and fraternity with mankind, and the direction of all our means and faculties to the purposes of improvement instead of destruction. With Europe we have few occasions of collision and these, with a little prudence and forbearance, may be generally accommodated. Of the brethren of our own hemisphere, none are yet, or for an age to come will be, in a shape, condition, or disposition to war against us. And the foothold which the nations of Europe had in either America, is slipping from under them, so that we shall soon be rid of their neighborhood.

III. ENGLAND

Revolt against British tyranny
To Randolph, 1775

Believe me, dear Sir, there is not in the British Empire a man who more cordially *loves* a union with Great Britain, than I do. But by the God that made me, I will cease to exist before I yield to a connection on such terms as the British Parliament proposes; and in this, I think I speak the sentiments of America. We want neither inducement nor power, to declare and assert a separation. It is will, alone, which is wanting, and that is growing apace under the fostering hand of our King. One bloody campaign will probably decide, everlastingly, our future course; and I am sorry to find a bloody campaign is decided on. If our winds and waters should not combine to rescue their shores from slavery, and General Howe's reinforcements should arrive in safety, we have hopes he will be inspirited to come out of Boston and take another drubbing; and we must drub him soundly, before the sceptered tyrant will know we are not mere brutes, to crouch under his hand, and kiss the rod with which he designs to scourge us.

To Randolph, 1775

I am sincerely one of those, and would rather be in dependence on Great Britain, properly limited, than on any nation on earth, or than on no nation. But I am one of those, too, who, rather than submit to the rights of legislating for us, assumed by the British Parliament, and which late experience has shown they will so cruelly exercise, would lend my hand to sink the whole Island in the ocean.

Why English policy is corrupt and perfidious
To J. Langdon, 1810

The Anglomen . . . have found [it] much safer . . . that we should first let England plunder us, as she has been doing for years, for fear Bonaparte should do it; and then ally ourselves with her, and enter into the war. . . . And what is to be our security, that when embarked for her in the war, she will . . . not leave us in the lurch? Her good faith! The faith of a nation of merchants! The *Punica fides* of modern Carthage! Of the friend and protectress of Copenhagen!* Of the nation who never admitted a chapter of morality into her political code! And is boldly avowing that whatever power can make hers, is hers of right. Money, and not morality, is the principle of commerce and commercial nations. But, in addition to this, the nature of the English government forbids, of itself, reliance on her engagements; and it is well known she has been the least faithful to her alliances of any na-

* In 1809 the British fleet, without warning and without declaration of war, bombarded Copenhagen and seized the Danish fleet.—*Editor.*

tion of Europe, since the period of her history wherein she has been distinguished for her commerce and corruption. . . .

It may be asked, what, in the nature of her government, unfits England for the observation of moral duties? In the first place, her King is a cypher; his only function being to name the oligarchy which is to govern her. The parliament is, by corruption, the mere instrument of the will of the administration. The real power and property in the government is in the great aristocratical families of the nation. The nest of office being too small for all of them to cuddle into at once, the contest is eternal, which shall crowd the other out. For this purpose, they are divided into two parties, the Ins and the Outs, so equal in weight that a small matter turns the balance. To keep themselves in, when they are in, every stratagem must be practised, every artifice used which may flatter the pride, the passions or power of the nation. Justice, honor, faith must yield to the necessity of keeping themselves in place. The question whether a measure is moral, is never asked; but whether it will nourish the avarice of their merchants, or the piratical spirit of their navy, or produce any other effect which may strengthen them in their places.

As to engagements, however positive, entered into by the predecessors of the Ins, why, they were their enemies; they did everything which was wrong; and to reverse everything which they did, must, therefore, be right. This is the true character of the English government in practice, however different its theory; and it presents the singular phenomenon of a nation, the individuals of which are as faithful to their private engagements and duties, as honorable, as worthy, as those of any nation on earth, and whose government is yet the most unprincipled at this day known.

To Rodney, 1810

The hurricane which is now blasting the world, physical and moral, has prostrated all the mounds of reason as well as right. . . . And when is this state of things to end? The death of Bonaparte would, to be sure, remove the first and chiefest apostle of the desolation of men and morals, and might withdraw the scourge of the land. But what is to restore order and safety on the ocean? The death of George III? Not at all. He is only stupid; and his ministers, however weak and profligate in morals, are ephemeral. But his nation is permanent, and it is that which is the tyrant of the ocean.

The principle that force is right, is become the principle of the nation itself.

Commerce and corrupt government have rotted the English
To Ogilvie, 1811

The English have been a wise, a virtuous and truly estimable people. But commerce and a corrupt government have rotted them to the core. Every generous, nay, every just sentiment, is absorbed in the thirst for gold. I speak of their cities, which we may certainly pronounce to be ripe for despotism, and fitted for no other government. Whether the leaven of the agricultural body is sufficient to regenerate the residuary mass, and maintain it in a sound state, under any reformation of government, may well be doubted.

Corruption of the English state
To J. F. Watson, 1814

It is not in the history of modern England or among the advocates of the principles or practices of her government, that the friend of freedom, or of political morality, is to seek instruction. There has indeed been a period, during which both were to be found, not in her government, but in the band of worthies who so boldly and ably reclaimed the rights of the people, and wrested from their government theoretic acknowledgments of them. This period began with the Stuarts, and continued but one reign after them. Since that, the vital principle of the English constitution is *corruption,* its practices the natural results of that principle, and their consequences a pampered aristocracy, annihilation of the substantial middle class, a degraded populace, oppressive taxes, general pauperism, and national bankruptcy.

England—a menace to America and the world
To Mme. de Staël, 1813

To complete and universalize the desolation of the globe, it has been the will of Providence to raise up, at the same time, a tyrant as unprincipled and as overwhelming, for the ocean. Not in the poor maniac George, but in his government and nation. Bonaparte will die, and his tyrannies with him. But a nation never dies. The English government, and its piratical principles and practices, have no fixed term of duration. Europe feels, and is writhing under the scorpion whips of Bonaparte. We are assailed by those of England. . . . The object of England is the *permanent domination of the ocean,* and the *monopoly of the trade of the world*. To secure this, she must keep a larger fleet than her own resources will maintain. The resources of other nations, then, must be impressed to supply the deficiency of her own.

Counter-revolutionary and anti-democratic English policy
To Governor Plumer, 1815

When England took alarm lest France, become republican, should recover energies dangerous to her, she employed emissaries with means to engage incendiaries and anarchists in the disorganization of all government there. These, assuming exaggerated zeal for republican government and the rights of the people, crowded their inscriptions into the Jacobin societies, and overwhelming by their majorities the honest and enlightened patriots of the original institution, distorted its objects, pursued its genuine founders under the name of Brissotines and Girondists unto death, intrigued themselves into the municipality of Paris, controlled by terrorism the proceedings of the legislature, in which they were faithfully aided by their co-stipendiaries there, the Dantons and Marats of the Mountain, murdered their king, septembrized the nation, and thus accomplished their stipulated task of demolishing liberty and government with it.

England now fears the rising force of this republican nation, and by the same means is endeavoring to effect the same course of miseries and destruction here; it is impossible where one sees like courses of events commence, not to ascribe them to like causes. We know that the government of England, maintaining itself by corruption at home, uses the same means in other countries of which she has any jealousy, by subsidizing agitators and traitors among themselves to distract and paralyze them.

Hostile to English injuries, but not to the people
To Rodney, 1815

I hope in God she [England] will change. There is not a nation on the globe with whom I have more earnestly wished a friendly intercourse on equal conditions. On no other would I hold out the hand of friendship to any. I know that their creatures represent me as personally an enemy to England. But fools only can believe this, or those who think me a fool. I am an enemy to her insults and injuries. I am an enemy to the flagitious principles of her administration, and to those which govern her conduct towards other nations. But would she give to morality some place in her political code, and especially would she exercise decency, and at least neutral passions towards us, there is not, I repeat it, a people on earth with whom I would sacrifice so much to be in friendship. They can do us, as enemies, more harm than any other nation; and in peace and in war, they have more means of disturbing us internally.

English corruption—a warning to America
To Logan, 1816

The man who is dishonest as a statesman would be a dishonest man in any station. It is strangely absurd to suppose that a million of human beings collected together are not under the same moral laws which bind each of them separately. It is a great consolation to me that our government, as it cherishes most its duties to its own citizens, so is it the most exact in its moral conduct towards other nations. . . . No voluntary wrong can be imputed to us. In this respect England exhibits the most remarkable phænomenon in the universe in the contrast between the profligacy of its government and the probity of its citizens. And accordingly it is now exhibiting an example of the truth of the maxim that virtue and interest are inseparable. It ends, as might have been expected, in the ruin of its people, but this ruin will fall heaviest, as it ought to fall, on the hereditary aristocracy which has for generations been preparing the catastrophe. I hope we shall take warning from the example and crush in its birth the aristocracy of our monied corporations which dare already to challenge our government to a trial of strength and bid defiance to the laws of our country.

IV. France

Criticism of French life and morals
To Bellini, 1785

Behold me at length on the vaunted scene of Europe! It is not necessary for your information, that I should enter into details concerning it. But you are, perhaps, curious to know how this new scene has struck a savage of the mountains of America. Not advantageously, I assure you. I find the general fate of humanity here most deplorable. The truth of Voltaire's observation, offers itself perpetually, that every man here must be either the hammer or the anvil. It is a true picture of that country to which they say we shall pass hereafter, and where we are to see God and his angels in splendor, and crowds of the damned trampled under their feet. While the great mass of the people are thus suffering under physical and moral oppression, I have endeavored to examine more nearly the condition of the great, to appreciate the true value of the circumstances, in their situation, which dazzle the bulk of spectators, and, especially, to compare it with that degree of happiness which is enjoyed in America, by every class of people. Intrigues of love occupy the younger, and those of ambition, the elder part of the great. Conjugal love having no existence among them, domestic happiness, of which that is the basis, is utterly unknown. In lieu of this, are substituted pursuits which nourish and invigorate all our bad passions, and which offer only moments of ecstasy, amidst days and months of restlessness and torment. Much, very much inferior, this, to the tranquil, permanent felicity with which domestic society in America blesses most of its inhabitants; leaving them to follow steadily those pursuits which health and reason approve, and rendering truly delicious the intervals of those pursuits.

What is admirable in French civilization
To Bellini, 1785

In the pleasure of the table, they are far before us, because, with good taste they unite temperance. They do not terminate the most sociable meals by transforming themselves into brutes. I have never yet seen a man drunk in France, even among the lowest of the people. Were I to proceed to tell you how much I enjoy their architecture, sculpture, painting, music, I should want words. It is in these arts they shine. The last of them, particularly, is an enjoyment, the deprivation of which with us, cannot be calculated. I am almost ready to say, it is the only thing which from my heart I envy them, and which, in spite of all the authority of the Decalogue, I do covet.

Concentration of property causes great misery in France
To Madison, 1785

[On my walk to Fontainebleau] as soon as I had got clear of the town I fell in with a poor woman walking at the same rate with myself and going the same course. Wishing to know the condition of the laboring poor I entered into conversation with her . . . [I] proceeded to enquire into her vocation, condition and circumstances. She told me she was a day laborer, at 8 sous or 4 pence sterling the day; that she had two children to maintain, and to pay a rent of 30 livres for her house (which would consume the hire of 75 days), that often she could get no emploiment, and of course was without bread. As we had walked together near a mile . . . , I gave her, on parting, 24 sous. She burst into tears of gratitude. . . .

This led me into a train of reflections on that unequal division of property which occasions the numberless instances of wretchedness which I had observed in this country and . . . all over Europe. The property of this country is absolutely concentrated in a very few hands. . . . These employ the flower of the country as servants (some as many as 200 domestics). . . . The most numerous of all classes, that is, the poor, cannot find work. I asked myself what could be the reason that so many should be permitted to beg who are willing to work, in a country where there is a very considerable proportion of uncultivated lands? . . . I am conscious that an equal division of property is impracticable. But the consequences of this enormous inequality producing so much misery to the bulk of mankind, legislators cannot invent too many devices for subdividing property. . . . The earth is given as a common stock for man to labour and live on. . . . It is not too soon to provide by every possible means that as few as possible shall be without a little portion of land. The small land holders are the most precious part of a state.

French wretchedness due to bad government
To Mrs. Trist, 1785

Yet, fallacious as the pursuits of happiness are, they seem on the whole to furnish the most effectual abstraction from a a contemplation of the hardness of their government. Indeed, it is difficult to conceive how so good a people, with so good a King, so well-disposed rulers in general, so genial a climate, so fertile a soil, should be rendered so ineffectual for producing human happiness by one single curse,—that of a bad form of government. But it is a fact, in spite of the mildness of their governors, the people are ground to powder by the vices of the form of government. Of twenty millions of people supposed to be in France, I am of opinion there are nineteen millions more wretched, more accursed in every circumstance of human existence than the most conspicuously wretched individual of the whole United States. I beg your pardon for getting into politics.

American Revolution stirred French minds
To Dr. Price, 1789

Yet the American war seems first to have awakened the thinking part of this nation in general from the sleep of despotism in which they were sunk. The officers too who had been to America, were mostly young men, less shackled by habit and prejudice, and more ready to assent to the dictates of common sense and common right. They came back impressed with these. The press, notwithstanding its shackles, began to disseminate them; conversation, too, assumed new freedom; politics became the theme of all societies, male and female, and a very extensive and zealous party was formed, which may be called the Patriotic party, who, sensible of the abusive government under which they lived, longed for occasions of reforming it. This party comprehended all the honesty of the kingdom, sufficiently at its leisure to think; the men of letters, the easy bourgeois, the young nobility, partly from reflection, partly from mode; for those sentiments became a matter of mode, and as such united most of the young women to the party.

Success of the French Revolution will influence the American
To Rutledge, 1791

I still hope the French revolution will issue happily. I feel that the permanence of our own, leans in some degree on that; and that a failure there would be a powerful argument to prove there must be a failure here.

To Mason, 1791

I look with great anxiety for the firm establishment of the new government in France, being perfectly convinced that if it takes place there, it will spread sooner or later all over Europe. On the contrary, a check there would retard the revival of liberty in other countries. I consider the establishment and success of their government as necessary to stay up our own, and to prevent it from falling back to that kind of half-way house, the English constitution.

Hopes that the French Revolution will spread
To Sinclair, 1791

We are now under the first impression of the news of the King's flight from Paris, and his recapture. It would be unfortunate were it in the power of any one man to defeat the issue of so beautiful a revolution. I hope and trust it is not, and that, for the good of suffering humanity all over the earth, that revolution will be established and spread through the whole world.

To T. Coxe, 1794

Over the foreign powers I am convinced they [the French people] will triumph completely, and I cannot but hope that that triumph, and the consequent disgrace of the invading tyrants, is destined, in order of events, to kindle the wrath of the people of Europe against those who have dared to embroil them in such wickedness, and to bring at length, kings, nobles and priests to the scaffolds which they have been so long deluging with human blood. I am still warm whenever I think of these scoundrels, though I do it as seldom as I can, preferring infinitely to contemplate the tranquil growth of my lucerne and potatoes.

Despite Revolution, treaty with France is binding
Opinion on . . . whether the United States have a right to renounce their treaties with France, April 28, 1793

The republic of the United States allied itself with France when under a despotic government. She changes her government, and declares it shall be a republic; prepares a form of republic extremely free, and in the meantime is governing herself as such. And it is proposed that America shall declare the treaties void, because it may say with truth that it would not have allied itself with that nation if it had been under the present form of its government. Who is the American who can say with truth that he would not have allied himself to France if she had been a republic? Or that a republic of any form would be as *disagreeable* as her ancient despotism? . . . I conclude, that the treaties are still binding, notwithstanding the change of government in France.

Bonaparte—a mass murderer
To Mme. de Staël, 1813

The day will come when a just posterity will give to their hero [Bonaparte] the only preëminence he has earned, that of having been the greatest of the destroyers of the human race. What year of his military life has not consigned a million of human beings to death, to poverty and wretchedness! What field in Europe may not raise a monument of the murders, the burnings, the desolations, the famines and miseries it has witnessed from him!

France will yet be free

To Paganel, 1811

We... weep over the fatal errors which have lost to nations the present hope of liberty, and to reason the fairest prospect of its final triumph over all imposture, civil and religious.... Shall we ever see as free and faithful a tableau of subsequent acts of this deplorable tragedy? [The counter-revolution in France.] Is reason to be forever amused with the *hochets* of physical sciences, in which she is indulged merely to divert her from solid speculations on the rights of man, and wrongs of his oppressors? It is impossible. The day of deliverance will come, although I shall not live to see it. The art of printing secures us against the retrogradation of reason and information, the examples of its safe and wholesome guidance in government, which will be exhibited through the widespread regions of the American continent, will obliterate, in time, the impressions left by the abortive experiment of France. With my prayers for the hastening of that auspicious day....

To B. Austin, 1816

That nation [France] is too high-minded, has too much innate force, intelligence and elasticity, to remain under its present compression. Samson will arise in his strength, as of old, and as of old will burst asunder the withes and the cords, and the webs of the Philistines. But what are to be the scenes of havoc and horror, and how widely they may spread between brethren of the same house, our ignorance of the interior feuds and antipathies of the country places beyond our ken.

It will end, nevertheless, in a representative government, in a government in which the will of the people will be an effective ingredient. This important element has taken root in the European mind, and will have its growth; their despots, sensible of this, are already offering this modification of their governments, as if of their own accord.

Instead of the parricide treason of Bonaparte, in perverting the means confided to him as a republican magistrate, to the subversion of that republic and erection of a military despotism for himself and his family, had he used it honestly for the establishment and support of a free government in his own country, France would now have been in freedom and rest; and her example operating in a contrary direction, every nation in Europe would have had a government over which the will of the people would have had some control.

His atrocious egotism has checked the salutary progress of principle, and deluged it with rivers of blood which are not yet run out. To the vast sum of devastation and of human misery, of which he has been the guilty cause, much is still to be added. But the object is fixed in the eye of nations, and they will press on to its accomplishment and to the general amelioration of the condition of man. What a germ have we planted, and how faithfully should we cherish the parent tree at home!

V. SOUTH AMERICA

God send them deliverance!
To Kosciuszko, 1811

And behold! another example of man rising in his might and bursting the chains of his oppressor, and in the same hemisphere. Spanish America is all in revolt. The insurgents are triumphant in many of the States, and will be so in all. But there the danger is that the cruel arts of their oppressors have enchained their minds, have kept them in the ignorance of children, and as incapable of self-government as children. If the obstacles of bigotry and priestcraft can be surmounted, we may hope that common sense will suffice to do everything else. God send them a safe deliverance.

Hopes for South American independence
To Lafayette, 1813

I join . . . sincerely . . . in wishes for the emancipation of South America. That they will be liberated from foreign subjection I have little doubt. But the result of my inquiries does not authorize me to hope they are capable of maintaining a free government. Their people are immersed in the darkest ignorance, and brutalized by bigotry and superstition. Their priests make of them what they please, and tho' they may have some capable leaders, yet nothing but intelligence in the people themselves can keep these faithful to their charge. Their efforts I fear therefore will end in establishing military despotisms in the several provinces. Among these there can be no confederacy. A republic of kings is impossible. But their future wars and quarrels among themselves will oblige them to bring the people into motion, into action, and into the exertion of their understandings. Light will at length beam in on their minds and the standing example we shall hold up, serving as an excitement as well as a model for their direction, may in the long run qualify them for self-government. This is the most I am able to hope for them. For I lay it down as one of the impossibilities of nature that ignorance should maintain itself free against cunning.

Keep Europe out of the American hemisphere
To Dr. Crawford, 1812

We especially ought to pray that the powers of Europe may be so poised and counterpoised among themselves, that their own safety may require the presence of all their force at home, leaving the other quarters of the globe in undisturbed tranquillity. When our strength will permit us to give the law of our hemisphere, it should be that the meridian of the mid-Atlantic should be the line of demarkation between war and peace, on this side of which no act of hostility should be committed, and the lion and the lamb lie down in peace together.

To Von Humboldt, 1813

History, I believe, furnishes no example of a priest-ridden people maintaining a free civil government. . . . The vicinity of New Spain to the United States, and their consequent intercourse, may furnish schools for the higher, and example for the lower classes of their citizens. And Mexico . . . may revolutionize itself under better auspices than the Southern provinces. These last, I fear, must end in military despotism. The different casts of their inhabitants, their mutual hatreds and jealousies, their profound ignorance and bigotry, will be played off by cunning leaders, and each be made the instrument of enslaving the others. . . . But in whatever government they end they will be *American* governments, no longer to be involved in the never-ceasing broils of Europe.

The European nations constitute a separate division of the globe; their localities make them part of a distinct system; they have a set of interests of their own in which it is our business never to engage ourselves. America has a hemisphere to itself. It must have its separate system of interests, which must not be subordinated to those of Europe. The insulated state in which nature has placed the American continent, should so far avail it that no spark of war kindled in the other quarters of the globe should be wafted across the wide oceans which separate us from them. And it will be so. In fifty years more the United States alone will contain fifty millions of inhabitants,* and fifty years are soon gone over.

Ignorance in South America may keep the people enslaved
To Dupont de Nemours, 1811

I fear the degrading ignorance into which their priests and kings have sunk them, has disqualified them from the maintenance or even knowledge of their rights, and that much blood may be shed for little improvement in their condition. Should their new rulers honestly lay their shoulders to remove the great obstacles of ignorance, and press the remedies of education and information, they will still be in jeopardy until another generation comes into place, and what may happen in the interval cannot be predicted, nor shall you or I live to see it.

To Lafayette, 1817

I wish I could give better hopes to our southern brethren. The achievement of their independence of Spain is no longer a question. But it is a very serious one, what will then become of them? Ignorance and bigotry, like other insanities, are incapable of self-government. They will fall under military despotism, and become the murderous tools of the ambition of their respective Bonapartes; and whether this will be for their greater happiness, the rule of one only has taught you to judge. No one, I hope, can doubt my wish to see them and all mankind exercising self-government, and capable of exercising it. But the question is not what we wish, but what is practicable? As their sincere friend and brother then, I do believe the best thing for them, would be for themselves to come to an accord with Spain, under the guarantee of France, Russia, Holland, and the United States, allowing to Spain a nominal supremacy, with authority only to keep the peace among them, leaving them otherwise all the powers of self-government, until their experience in them, their emancipation from their priests, and advancement in information, shall prepare them for complete independence. I exclude England from this confederacy, because her selfish principles render her incapable of honorable patronage or disinterested cooperation; unless, indeed, what seems now probable, a revolution should restore to her an honest government, one which will permit the world to live in peace.

* Jefferson's prophecy proved nearly correct. In 1870 there were almost 40,000,000 people in the United States; in 1880, 50,000,000; and in 1920, over 120,000,000.—*Editor.*

To Destutt de Tracy, 1820: N. Y. Pub. Lib., MS, V, 12-13

In the meantime we receive and protect the flag of South America in its commercial intercourse with us. . . . And if we should not be the first, we shall certainly be the second nation in acknowledging the entire independence of our new friends. What that independence will end in, I fear is problematical. Whether in wise government or military despotism. But prepared, however, or not for self-government, if it is their will to make the trial, it is our duty and desire to wish it cordially success, and of ultimate success there can be no doubt.

Essential unity of all the Americas
To a friend—(?), 1820: N. Y. Pub. Lib., MS, IV, 490

I hope . . . [for] a cordial fraternization among all the American nations, and . . . their coalescing in an American system of policy, totally independent of, and unconnected with that of Europe. The day is not distant when we may formally require a meridian of partition thro' the ocean which separates the two hemispheres, on the hither side of which no European gust shall ever be heard, nor an American on the other; and when during the rage of the eternal wars of Europe, the lion and the lamb within our regions shall lie down together in peace. The surplus of population in Europe and want of room render war, in their opinion, necessary to keep down their excess numbers. Here, room is abundant, population scanty, and peace the necessary state for producing men to whom the redundant soil is offering the means of life and happiness. The principles of society then, there and here, are radically different. and I hope no American patriot will ever lose sight of the essential policy of interdicting in the seas and territories of both Americas, the ferocious and sanguinary contests of Europe. . . . I should rejoice to see the fleets of Brazil and the United States riding together as brethren of the same family and having the same interests.

Should the United States take Spanish provinces?
To President Monroe, 1823

But we have first to ask ourselves a question. Do we wish to acquire to our own confederacy any one or more of the Spanish provinces? I candidly confess, that I have ever looked on Cuba as the most interesting addition which could ever be made to our system of States. The control which, with Florida Point, this island would give us over the Gulf of

Mexico, and the countries and isthmus bordering on it, as well as those whose waters flow into it, would fill up the measure of our political well-being. Yet, as I am sensible that this can never be obtained, even with her own consent, but by war; and its independence, which is our second interest (and especially its independence of England) can be secured without it, I have no hesitation in abandoning my first wish to future chances, and accepting its independence, with peace and the friendship of England, rather than its association, at the expense of war and her enmity.

APPENDIX I

AXIOMS AND DICTA

The principles of Jefferson are the definitions and axioms of a free society.—ABRAHAM LINCOLN, 1859.

EDUCATION

No one more sincerely wishes the spread of information among mankind than I do, and none has greater confidence in its effect towards supporting free and good government. (*To Hugh L. White, et al., 1810.*)

If a nation expects to be ignorant and free, in a state of civilization, it expects what never was and never will be. (*To Colonel Yancey, 1816.*)

The brier and bramble can never become the vine and olive; but their asperities may be softened by culture, and their properties improved to usefulness. . . . In the present spirit of extending to the great mass of mankind the blessings of instruction, I see a prospect of great advancement in the happiness of the human race. (*To Cornelius C. Blatchly, 1822.*)

ENGLAND

[England] never admitted a chapter of morality in her political code. (*To J. Langdon, 1810.*)

It is well known she has been the least faithful to her alliances of any nation of Europe. (*Ibid.*)

[England] presents the singular phenomenon of a nation, the individuals of which are as faithful to their private engagements and duties, as honorable, as worthy, as those of any nation on earth, and whose government is yet the most unprincipled at this day known. *(Ibid.)*

The English hate us because they think our prosperity filched from theirs. (*To Colonel Duane, 1810.*)

The modern Carthage will end as the old one has done. I am sorry for her [England's] people, who are individually as respectable as those of other nations—it is her government which is so corrupt, and which has destroyed the nation—it was certainly the most corrupt and unprincipled government on earth. (*Ibid.*)

The object of England is the *permanent dominion of the ocean*, and the *monopoly of the trade of the world*. (*To Mme. de Staël, 1813.*)

England [is] a nation of pikes and gudgeons, the latter bred merely as food for the former. (*To Monroe, 1815.*)

[England's] selfish principles render her incapable of honorable patronage or disinterested coöperation. (*To Lafayette, 1817.*)

EQUALITY

Our ancestors who migrated hither were laborers, not lawyers. (*Rights of British America, 1774.*)

An aristocracy of wealth [is] of more harm and danger than benefit to society. (*Autobiography, 1821.*)

There is a natural aristocracy among men. The grounds of this are virtue and talents. . . . The natural aristocracy I consider as the most precious gift of nature, for the instruction, the trusts, and government of society. (*To Adams, 1813.*)

We hold these truths to be self-evident: that all men are created equal; that they are endowed by their Creator with inherent and unalienable rights; that among these are life, liberty, and the pursuit of happiness. (*Declaration of Independence, 1776.*)

Men by their constitution are naturally divided into two parties. Those who fear and distrust the people. . . . Those who identify themselves with the people, have confidence in them, cherish and consider them as the most honest & safe . . . depository of the public interest. (*To H. Lee, 1824.*)

An industrious farmer occupies a more dignified place in the scale of beings . . . than a lazy lounger, valuing himself on his family, too proud to work, and drawing out a miserable existence by eating on that surplus of other men's labor, which is the sacred fund of the helpless poor. (*To De Meunier, 1786.*)

I am ready to say to every human being 'thou art my brother' and to offer him the hand of concord and amity. *(To Brazer, 1819: N. Y. Pub. Lib., MS, V, 142.)*

Foreign Affairs

Commerce with all nations, alliance with none, should be our motto. *(To T. Lomax, 1799.)*

I am not for linking ourselves by new treaties with the quarrels of Europe; entering that field of slaughter to preserve their balance, or joining in the confederacy of kings to war against the principles of liberty. *(To Elbridge Gerry, 1799.)*

We have a perfect horror at everything like connecting ourselves with the politics of Europe. *(To William Short, 1801.)*

And would we accept the infamy of France or England in exchange for our honest reputation . . . , in exchange for the prosperity, the freedom and independence which we have preserved safely through the wreck? *(To Eppes, 1811.)*

The insulated state in which nature has placed the American continent, should so far avail it that no spark of war kindled in the other quarters of the globe should be wafted across the wide oceans which separate us from them. *(To Baron von Humboldt, 1813.)*

Peace and friendship with all mankind is our wisest policy. *(To Dumas, 1786.)*

I have ever deemed it fundamental for the United States, never to take active part in the quarrels of Europe. Their political interests are entirely distinct from ours. . . . They are nations of eternal war. *(To President Monroe, 1823.)*

Our first and fundamental maxim should be, never to entangle ourselves in the broils of Europe. Our second, never to suffer Europe to intermeddle with cis-Atlantic affairs. *(Ibid.)*

It was not expected in this age, that nations so honorably distinguished by their advances in science and civilization, would suddenly cast away the esteem they had merited from the world, and, revolting from the empire of morality, assume a character in history, which all the tears of their posterity will never wash from its pages. *(To the Democratic Republican Delegates of Philadelphia, 1808.)*

Peace, commerce, and honest friendship, with all nations—entangling alliances with none. *(First Inaugural, 1801.)*

JUDICIARY

It is a misnomer to call a government republican, in which a branch of the supreme power is independent of the nation. *(To Pleasants, 1821.)*

The judiciary of the United States is the subtle corps of sappers and miners constantly working under the ground to undermine the foundations of our confederated fabric.
A judiciary independent of a king or executive alone, is a good thing; but independence of the will of the nation is a solecism, at least in a republican government. *(To Ritchie, 1820.)*

To consider the judges as the ultimate arbiters of all constitutional questions [is] a very dangerous doctrine indeed, and one which would place us under the despotism of an oligarchy. . . . The Constitution has erected no such single tribunal. *(To W. C. Jarvis, 1820.)*

The great object of my fear is the Federal Judiciary. That body, like gravity, ever acting, with noiseless foot, and alarming advance . . . , is engulfing insidiously the special governments into the jaws of that which feeds them. *(To Judge Roane, 1821.)*

But the opinion which gives to the judges the right to decide what laws are constitutional, and what not, not only for themselves in their own sphere of action, but for the Legislature and executive also, in their spheres, would make the judiciary a despotic branch. *(To Abigail Adams, 1804.)*

LAW AND THE CONSTITUTION

[*The Federalist*] is the best commentary on the principles of government which ever was written. *(To Madison, 1788.)*

The execution of the laws is more important than the making them. *(To Arnoud, 1789.)*

No society can make a perpetual constitution, or even a perpetual law. *(To Madison, 1789.)*

The difficulty with us is how to bring the guilty to punishment, and not how to oppress the innocent. *(To Ch. Clarke, 1816: N. Y. Pub. Lib., MS, IV, 399.)*

I formally combatted [the] heretical doctrine that the judiciary is the ultimate expounder and arbiter of all constitutional questions. *(To Thweatt, 1821: ibid., V, 38.)*

The machine [Constitution], as it is, will, I believe, last my time, and those coming after will know how to repair it to their own minds. *(To Pleasants, 1821.)*

Some men look at constitutions with sanctimonious reverence and deem them like the ark of the covenant, too sacred to be touched. . . . But I know also that laws and institutions must go hand in hand with the progress of the human mind. *(To Kercheval, 1816.)*

The Constitution of the United States [is] the result of the collected wisdom of our country. *(To A. Marsh, 1801: N. Y. Pub. Lib., MS, II, 84.)*

Though written constitutions may be violated in moments of passion or delusion, yet they furnish a text to which those who are watchful may again rally and recall the people; they fix too for the people the principles of their political creed. *(To Dr. Priestley, 1802.)*

The Constitution of the United States is a compact of independent nations subject to the rules acknowledged in similar cases. *(To Edward Everett, 1826.)*

Liberty

The God who gave us life, gave us liberty at the same time: the hand of force may destroy, but cannot disjoin them.

For a people who are free and who mean to remain so, a well-organized and armed militia is their best security. *(Eighth Annual Message, 1808.)*

A naval force can never endanger our liberties, nor occasion bloodshed; a land force would do both. *(To Monroe, 1786.)*

I would rather be exposed to the inconveniences attending

too much liberty, than those attending too small a degree of it. *(To A. Stuart, 1791.)*

I may err in my measures, but never shall deflect from the *intention* to fortify the public liberty by every possible means, and to put it out of the power of the few to riot on the labors of the many. *(To Judge Tyler, 1804: N. Y. Pub. Lib., MS, III, 33.)*

This ball of liberty, I believe most piously, is now so well in motion that it will roll round the globe, at least the enlightened part of it, for light and liberty go together. *(To T. Coxe, 1795.)*

There are rights which it is useless to surrender to the government, and which governments have yet always been found to invade. These are the rights of thinking, and publishing our thoughts by speaking or writing; the right of free commerce; the right of personal freedom. *(To Humphreys, 1789.)*

The ground of liberty is to be gained by inches, we must be contented to secure what we can get, from time to time, and eternally press forward for what is yet to get. It takes time to persuade men to do even what is for their own good. *(To Ch. Clay, 1790.)*

The natural progress of things is for liberty to yield and government to gain ground. *(To Carrington, 1788.)*

The freedom and happiness of man . . . are the sole objects of all legitimate government. *(To Kosciuszko, 1810.)*

Reformation is more practicable by operating on the mind than on the body of man. *(To Paine, 1792.)*

To attain all this [liberty in European countries], rivers of blood must yet flow, and years of desolation pass over; yet the object is worth rivers of blood and years of desolation. *(To Adams, 1823.)*

Opinion, and the just maintenance of it, shall never be a crime in my view: nor bring injury on the individual. *(To Samuel Adams, 1801.)*

Timid men . . . prefer the calm of despotism to the boisterous sea of liberty. *(To Mazzei, 1796.)*

I tolerate with the utmost latitude the right of others to differ from me in opinion. *(To Abigail Adams, 1804.)*

When I hear another express an opinion which is not mine, I say to myself, he has a right to his opinion, as I to mine; why should I question it? His error does me no injury, and shall I become a Don Quixote, to bring all men by force of argument to one opinion? *(To Thomas Jefferson Randolph, 1808.)*

History, I believe, furnishes no example of a priest-ridden people maintaining a free civil government. *(To Baron von Humboldt, 1813.)*

I fear nothing for our liberty from the assaults of force; but I have seen and felt much, and fear more from English books, English prejudices, English manners, and the apes, the dupes, and designs among our professional crafts. *(To Horatio G. Spafford, 1814.)*

[If the book] be false in its facts, disprove them; if false in its reasoning, refute it. But, for God's sake, let us freely hear both sides. *(To Dufief, 1814.)*

What a germ have we planted, and how faithfully should we cherish the parent tree at home! *(To Benjamin Austin, 1816.)*

The boisterous sea of liberty indeed is never without a wave. *(To Lafayette, 1820.)*

The mass of mankind has not been born with saddles on their backs, nor a favored few booted and spurred, ready to ride them legitimately, by the grace of God. *(To Weightman, 1826.)*

I am not among those who fear the people. They, and not the rich, are our dependence for continued freedom. *(To Samuel Kercheval, 1816.)*

Sole depositories of the remains of human liberty, our duty to ourselves, to posterity, and to mankind, call on us by every motive which is sacred or honorable, to watch over the safety of our beloved country during the troubles which agitate and convulse the residue of the world. *(To the Legislature of New York State, 1809.)*

Subject opinion to coercion: whom will you make your inquisitors? Fallible men; men governed by bad passions, by private as well as public reasons. *(Notes on Virginia, Query 17.)*

Monarchy

No race of kings has ever presented above one man of common sense in twenty generations. *(To Hawkins, 1787.)*

With all the defects of our constitution . . ., the comparison of our governments with those of Europe, is like a comparison of heaven and hell. *(To Joseph Jones, 1787.)*

There is scarcely an evil known in these [European] countries which may not be traced to their kings. *(To Washington, 1788.)*

There is not a crowned head in Europe, whose talents or merits would entitle him to be elected a vestryman by the people of any parish in America. *(Ibid.)*

To appoint a monarchist to conduct the affairs of a republic is like appointing an atheist to the priesthood. *(To General Gates, 1810: N. Y. Pub. Lib., MS, II, 6.)*

A republic of kings is impossible. *(To Lafayette, 1813: N. Y. Pub. Lib., MS, IV, 214-15.)*

Take any race of animals, confine them in idleness and inaction, whether in a stye, a stable or a state-room, pamper them with a high diet, gratify all their sexual appetites, immerse them in sensualities, nourish their passions, let everything bend before them, and banish whatever might lead them to think, and in a few generations they become all body and no mind. . . . Such is the regimen in raising kings. *(To J. Langdon, 1810.)*

Kings—from all of whom the Lord deliver us. *(Ibid.)*

Moral and Philosophic Maxims

To buy off one lie is to give a premium for the invention of others. *(To Wm. Burwell, 1808: N. Y. Pub. Lib., MS, IV, 45.)*

The man who fears no truths has nothing to fear from lies. *(To Logan, 1816: ibid., IV, 375.)*

Virtue and interest are inseparable. *(To Logan, 1816: ibid., IV, 411.)*

APPENDIX I

Men in glass houses should not provoke a war of stones. *(To R. Walsh, 1820.)*

There is a time for things; for advancing and for retiring; for a Sabbath of rest as well as for days of labor. *(To Thweatt, 1821: N. Y. Pub. Lib., MS, V, 38.)*

Maxims for the conduct of a young man:*
1. Never spend your money before you have it
2. Never buy what you don't want because it is cheap: it will be dear to you.
3. Pride costs more than hunger, thirst and cold
4. Never put off to-morrow what you can do to-day
5. Never trouble another for what you can do yourself
6. Think as you please and let others do so; you will then have no disputes
7. How much pain have cost us the things which have never happened
8. Take things always by their smooth handle
9. When angry count 10 before you speak. If very angry 100
10. When at table, remember that we never repent of having eaten or drunk too little. *(To Charles Clay, 1817.)*

Public emploiment contributes neither to advantage nor to happiness. It is but honorable exile from ones family and affairs. *(To F. Willis, 1790.)*

I have no ambition to govern men. It is a painful and thankless office. *(To Adams, 1796.)*

The patriot, like the Christian, must learn that to bear revilings and persecutions is a part of his duty. *(To Judge Sullivan, 1805.)*

The second office of the government is honorable and easy, the first is but a splendid misery. *(To Elbridge Gerry, 1797.)*

Blest is that nation whose silent course of happiness furnishes nothing for history to say. This is what I ambition for my own country. *(To Comte Diodati, 1807.)*

What I value more than all things [is] good humor. *(To Doctor Rush, 1808.)*

Nothing betrays imbecility so much as the being insensible of it. *(Ibid., 1811.)*

---
* "I send a little bundle of canons of conduct which may merit a shelf after the one occupied by the Decalogue of first authority."

Merchants have no country. *(To Horatio G. Spafford, 1814.)*

No national crime passes unpunished in the long run. *(To De Marbois, 1817.)*

My theory has always been, that if we are to dream the flatteries of hope are as cheap, and pleasanter than the gloom of despair. *(Ibid.)*

No nation is drunken where wine is cheap; and none sober, where the dearness of wine substitutes ardent spirits as the common beverage. *(To De Neuville, 1818.)*

I deem it the duty of every man to devote a certain proportion of his income for charitable purposes. *(To Doctors Rogers and Slaughter, 1806.)*

Negro Slavery

To give liberty to, or rather, to abandon persons whose habits have been formed in slavery is like abandoning children. *(To E. Bancroft, 1789.)*

A man's moral sense must be unusually strong, if slavery does not make him a thief. He who is permitted by law to have no property of his own, can with difficulty conceive that property is founded in anything but force. *(Ibid.)*

No body wishes more than I do to see . . . proofs . . . that nature has given to our black brethren, talents equal to those of the other colors of men. *(To B. Banneker, 1791.)*

The love of justice and the love of country plead equally the cause of these people, and it is a moral reproach to us-that they should have pleaded it so long in vain. . . . Yet the hour of emancipation is advancing, in the march of time. *(To E. Coles, 1814.)*

The whole commerce between master and slave is a perpetual exercise of the most boisterous passions, the most unremitting despotism on the one part, and degrading submissions on the other. *(Notes on Virginia, Query 18)*

Political Economy

Agriculture, manufactures, commerce and navigation, the four pillars of our prosperity, are the most thriving when left most free to individual enterprise. *(First Annual Message, 1801.)*

The earth belongs to the living and not to the dead. *(To Madison, 1789.)*

We can pay off his [Hamilton's] debt in fifteen years, but we can never get rid of his financial system. *(To Dupont, 1802: N. Y. Pub. Lib., MS, II, 171.)*

The interests of the agriculturalist, the manufacturer, the merchant and the navigator are so intimately blended together, that to keep them all in just balance . . . requires a knowledge of facts, as well as possession of sound principles rarely to be found. *(To Lithgow, 1805: ibid., III, 217.)*

We consider ourselves unauthorized to saddle posterity with our debts. *(To—(?), 1813: ibid., IV, 194.)*

The only safe, the only lawful and honest [system of finance] consists of borrowing on such short terms of reimbursement of interest and principal, as will fall within the accomplishment of our own lives. *(Ibid., p. 196.)*

It is a kind of law of nature that every nation prospers by the prosperity of others. *(To Ticknor, 1816: ibid., IV, 339.)*

It is incumbent on every generation to pay its own debts as it goes. A principle which, if acted on, would save one half the wars of the world. *(To Destutt de Tracy, 1820.)*

Debt and revolution are inseparable as cause and effect. *(To Samuel Smith, 1821.)*

I think it a great error to consider a heavy tax on wines, as a tax on luxury. On the contrary it is a tax on the health of our citizens. It is a legislative declaration that none but the richest of them shall be permitted to drink wine, and in effect a condemnation of all the middling and lower conditions of society to the poison of whisky, which is destroying them by wholesale. *(To Crawford, 1818.)*

Legislators cannot invent too many devices for sub-dividing property. . . . The earth is given as a common stock for man to labor and live on. . . . The small land holders are the most precious part of a state. *(To Madison, 1785.)*

The greatest security against the introduction of corrupt practices and principles into our government is to make [them keep] . . . public expenses down to their minimum *(To Gallatin, 1804.)*

If the public debt should once more be swelled to a formidable size, . . . we shall be committed to the English career of debt, corruption and rottenness, closing with revolution. *(To Gallatin, 1809.)*

Every generous, nay, every just sentiment, is absorbed in the thirst for gold. *(To Ogilvie, 1811.)*

You might as well, with the sailors, whistle to the wind as suggest precautions against having too much money. *(To Adams, 1814.)*

No one has a natural right to the trade of a money lender, but he who has the money to lend. *(To John W. Eppes, 1813.)*

I place economy among the first and most important of republican virtues, and public debt as the greatest of the dangers to be feared. *(To Governor Plumer, 1816.)*

Those who labor in the earth are the chosen people of God, if ever He had a chosen people, whose breasts He has made His peculiar deposit for substantial and genuine virtue. *(Notes on Virginia, Query 19.)*

Generally speaking, the proportion which the aggregate of the other classes of citizens bears in any State to that of its husbandmen, is the proportion of its unsound to its healthy parts. *(Ibid.)*

Popular Government

I have such reliance on the good sense of the body of the people and the honesty of their leaders, that I am not afraid of their letting things go wrong to any length in any cause. *(To Dumas, 1788.)*

Whenever the people are well-informed, they can be trusted with their own government; whenever things get so far wrong as to attract their notice, they may be relied on to set them to rights. *(To Dr. Price, 1789.)*

Trial by jury, I consider as the only anchor ever yet imagined by man, by which a government can be held to the principles of its constitution. *(To Thomas Paine, 1789.)*

APPENDIX I

To introduce the people into every department of government . . . is the only way to insure a long-continued and honest administration. *(To Arnoud, 1789.)*

We have already given one effectual check to the dog of war, by transferring the power of declaring war from the executive to the legislative body, from those who are to spend to those who are to pay. *(To Madison, 1789.)*

Responsibility is a tremendous engine in a free government. *(To A. Stuart, 1791.)*

I have great confidence in the common sense of mankind in general. *(To J. Moor, 1800: N. Y. Pub. Lib., MS, I, 366.)*

The greatest good we can do our country is to heal its party divisions and make them one people. *(To J. Dickinson, 1801: ibid., II, 67.)*

I hold it therefore certain that to open the doors of truth and to fortify the habit of testing everything by reason, are the most effectual manacles we can rivet on the hands of our successors to prevent their manacling the people with their own consent. *(To Judge Tyler, 1804: ibid., III, 34.)*

He who would do his country the most good he can, must go quietly with the prejudices of the majority till he can lead them into reason. *(To Cæsar Rodney, 1805: ibid., III, 164-65.)*

I think we have more machinery of government than is necessary, too many parasites living on the labor of the industries. *(To W. Ludlow, 1824.)*

The will of the people is the only legitimate foundation of any government. *(To B. Waring, 1801.)*

I am not a friend to a very energetic government. It is always oppressive. *(To Madison, 1787.)*

Political dissension is . . . a less evil than the lethargy of despotism. *(To T. Pinckney, 1797.)*

I have been [unable] to conceive how any rational being could propose happiness to himself from the exercise of power over others. *(To De Tracy, 1811.)*

The sheep are happier of themselves, than under care of the wolves. *(Notes on Virginia, 1787 ed.)*

The time to guard against corruption and tyranny, is before they shall have gotten hold of us. It is better to keep the wolf out of the fold, than to trust to drawing his teeth and claws after he shall have entered. *(Ibid., Query 13.)*

Every government degenerates when trusted to the rulers . . . alone. The people themselves are its only safe depositories. *(Ibid., Query 14.)*

Nothing then is unchangeable but the inherent and inalienable rights of man. *(To Cartwright, 1824.)*

I know of no safe depository of the ultimate powers of the society but the people themselves. *(To Jarvis, 1821.)*

My most earnest wish is to see the republican element of popular control pushed to the maximum of its practicable exercise. I shall then believe that our government may be pure and perpetual. *(To I. H. Tiffany, 1816.)*

I do not indeed wish to see any nation have a form of government forced on them; but if it is to be done, I should rejoice at its being a free one. *(To Peregrine Fitzhugh, 1798.)*

We see the wisdom of Solon's remark, that no more good must be attempted than the nation can bear. *(To Dr. Walter Jones, 1801.)*

My conviction [is], that should things go wrong at any time, the people will set them to rights by the peaceable exercise of their elective rights. *(To Wilson C. Nicholas, 1806.)*

There is a snail-paced gate for the advance of new ideas on the general mind, under which we must acquiesce. . . . You must give [the people] time for every step you take. *(To Barlow, 1807.)*

The only orthodox object of the institution of government is to secure the greatest degree of happiness possible to the general mass of those associated under it. *(To Van der Kemp, 1812.)*

No, my friend, the way to have good and safe government, is not to trust it all to one, but to divide it among the many. *(To Joseph C. Cabell, 1816.)*

We of the United States, you know, are constitutionally and conscientiously democrats. *(To Dupont de Nemours, 1816.)*

We both consider the people as our children. . . . But you love them as infants whom you are afraid to trust without nurses; and I as adults whom I freely leave to self-government. *(Ibid.)*

No government can continue good, but under the control of the people. *(To Adams, 1819.)*

When all government, domestic and foreign, in little as in great things, shall be drawn to Washington as the center of all power, it will render powerless the checks provided of one government on another, and will become as venal and oppressive as the government from which we separated. *(To C. Hammond, 1821.)*

Every man, and every body of men on earth, possesses the right of self-government. They receive it with their being from the hand of nature. Individuals exercise it by their single will; collections of men by that of their majority; for the law of the *majority* is the natural law of every society of men. *(Opinion upon the question whether . . . the seat of government shall be transferred to the Potomac, 1790.)*

Sometimes it is said that man cannot be trusted with the government of himself. Can he, then, be trusted with the government of others? Or have we found angels in the forms of kings to govern him? *(First Inaugural, 1801.)*

Believing that a representative government, responsible at short periods of election, is that which produces the greatest sum of happiness to mankind, I feel it a duty to do no act which shall essentially impair that principle. *(To the Legislature of Vermont, 1807.)*

The mobs of great cities add just so much to the support of pure government, as sores do to the strength of the human body. *(Notes on Virginia, Query 19.)*

Press

Man may be governed by reason and truth. Our first object should therefore be to leave open to him all the avenues to truth. The most effectual hitherto found is the freedom of the press. *(To Judge Tyler, 1804.)*

They [the Federalists] fill their newspapers with falsehoods, calumnies and audacities. . . . I shall protect them in the right of lying and calumniating. *(To Volney, 1802.)*

I have lent myself willingly as the subject of a great experiment . . . to demonstrate the falsehood of the pretext that freedom of the press is incompatible with orderly government. *(To Seymour, 1807.)*

The newspapers of our country by their abandoned spirit of falsehood, have more effectually destroyed the utility of the press than all the shackles devised by Bonaparte. *(To T. Wortman, 1813.)*

Our liberty depends on the freedom of the press, and that cannot be limited without being lost. *(To Dr. J. Currie, 1786.)*

To the press alone, chequered as it is with abuses, the world is indebted for all the triumphs which have been gained by reason and humanity over error and oppression . . .; to the same benefit source, the United States owe much of the lights which conducted them to the rank of a free and independent nation. *(Virginia and Kentucky Resolutions, 1799.)*

The press [is] the only tocsin of a nation. *(To Thomas Cooper, 1802.)*

Where the press is free, and every man able to read, all is safe. *(To Colonel Yancey, 1816.)*

This formidable censor of the public functionaries, by arranging them at the tribunal of public opinion, produces reform peaceably, which must otherwise be done by revolution. *(To Coray, 1823.)*

Public Morality

We are firmly convinced . . . that with nations, as with individuals, our interests soundly calculated, will ever be found inseparable from our moral duties. *(Second Inaugural, 1805.)*

To say that gratitude is never to enter into the motives of national conduct, is to revive a principle which has been buried for centuries with its kindred principles of the lawfulness of assassination, poison, perjury. *(To Madison, 1789.)*

He who says I will be a rogue when I act in company with a hundred others, but an honest man when I act alone, will be believed in the former assertion, but not in the later. *(Ibid.)*

I may further say that I have not observed men's honesty to increase with their riches. *(To J. Moor, 1800.)*

Never let *us* do wrong, because our opponents did so. Let us, rather, by doing right, show them what they ought to have done, and establish a rule the dictates of reason and conscience, rather than of the angry passions. *(To General Gates, 1801: N. Y. Pub. Lib., MS, II, p. 8.)*

No nation, however powerful, any more than an individual, can be unjust with impunity. Sooner or later public opinion, an instrument merely moral in the beginning, will find occasion physically to inflict its sentence on the unjust. *(To Madison, 1804.)*

The man who is dishonest as a statesman would be a dishonest man in any station. It is strangely absurd to suppose that a million of human beings collected together are not under the same moral laws which bind each of them separately. *(To Dr. G. Logan, 1816.)*

No man has a natural right to commit aggression on the equal rights of another. *(To Francis W. Gilmer, 1816.)*

Religion

I never had an opinion in politics or religion, which I was afraid to own. *(To Hopkinson, 1789.)*

Could the people of that State [Massachusetts] emerge from the deceptions under which they are kept by their clergy, lawyers and English presses, our salvation would be sure and easy. *(To E. Pendleton, 1799: N. Y. Pub. Lib., MS, I, 271.)*

The clergy, by getting themselves established by law and ingrafted into the machine of government, have been a very formidable engine against the civil and religious rights of man. *(To J. Moor, 1800: ibid., I, 366.)*

I have considered [religion] as a matter between every man and his maker, in which no other, and far less the public had a right to intermeddle. *(To Rush, 1813: ibid., IV, 164.)*

The way to silence religious disputes is to take no notice of them. *(Notes on Virginia.)*

The priests have so disfigured the simple religion of Jesus that no one who reads the sophistications they have engrafted on it . . . would conceive these could have been fathered on the sublime preacher of the Sermon on the Mount. *(To Dr. B. Waterhouse, 1815: N. Y. Pub. Lib., MS, IV, 2-3.)*

The sum of all religion as expressed by its best preacher, 'Fear God and love thy neighbor,' contains no mystery, needs no explanation. But this won't do. It gives no scope to make dupes; priests could not live by it. *(To Logan, 1816.)*

As usual, those whose dogmas are the most unintelligible are the most angry. *(To S. Hales, 1818: N. Y. Pub. Lib., MS, V, 79.)*

The truth is that Calvinism has introduced into the Christian religion more new absurdities than its leaders had purged it of old ones. *(Ibid.)*

Our Savior did not come into this world to save metaphysicians only. His doctrines are levelled to the simplest understanding, and it is only by banishing Hierophantic mysteries and Scholastic subtleties, which they have nicknamed Christianity, and getting back to the plain and unsophisticated precepts of Christ, that we become *real* Christians. *(Ibid.)*

It does me no injury for my neighbor to say there are twenty gods, or no God. It neither picks my pocket nor breaks my leg. *(Notes on Virginia, Query 17.)*

Is uniformity attainable? Millions of innocent men, women, and children, since the introduction of Christianity, have been burnt, tortured, fined, imprisoned; yet we have not advanced one inch towards uniformity. *(Ibid.)*

I consider the government of the United States as interdicted by the Constitutions from intermeddling with religious institutions. . . . I do not believe it is for the interest of religion to invite the civil magistrate to direct its exercises, its discipline, or its doctrines. *(To Rev. S. Miller, 1808.)*

Of all the systems of morality, ancient and modern, which have come under my observation, none appear to me so pure as that of Jesus. *(To W. Canby, 1813.)*

In all [religions] we see good men, and as many in one as another. *(To J. Fishback, 1809.)*

Ideas must be distinct before reason can act upon them; and no man ever had a distinct idea of the trinity. It is the mere Abracadabra of the mountebanks calling themselves the priests of Jesus. *(To Van der Kemp, 1816.)*

Three are one, and one is three; and yet the one is not three, and the three are not one. . . . This constitutes the craft, the power and the profit of the priests. Sweep away their gossamer fabrics of factious religion, and they would catch no more flies. *(To Adams, 1813.)*

It behoves every man who values liberty of conscience for himself, to resist invasions of it in the case of others. *(To Dr. Benjamin Rush, 1803.)*

I am a Christian, in the only sense in which he wished any one to be; sincerely attached to his doctrines, in preference to all others. *(Ibid.)*

I never will, by any word or act, bow to the shrine of intolerance, or admit a right on inquiry into the religious opinions of others. *(To Edward Dowse, 1803.)*

In every country and in every age, the priest has been hostile to liberty. He is always in alliance with the despot, abetting his abuses in return for protection of his own. *(To Horatio G. Spafford, 1814.)*

Our particular principles of religion are a subject of accountability to our God alone. I inquire after no man's, and trouble none with mine. *(To Miles King, 1814.)*

I have ever judged of the religion of others by their lives. . . . For it is in our lives, and not from our words, that our religion must be read. *(To Mrs. Harrison Smith, 1816.)*

My opinion is that there would never have been an infidel, if there had never been a priest. *(Ibid.)*

The metaphysical insanities of Athanasius, of Loyola, and of Calvin, are, to my understanding, mere lapses into polytheism, differing from paganism only by being more unintelligible. *(To Jared Sparks, 1820.)*

[Creeds] have been the bane and ruin of the Christian church . . . , made of Christendom a slaughter-house. *(To the Rev. Whittemore, 1822.)*

Had the doctrines of Jesus been preached always as pure as they came from his lips, the whole civilized world would now have been Christian. *(To Dr. Benjamin Waterhouse, 1822.)*

I think that every Christian sect gives a great handle to atheism by their general dogma that, without a revelation, there would not be sufficient proof of the being of a God. *(To Adams, 1823.)*

To compel a man to furnish contributions of money for the propagation of opinions which he disbelieves, is sinful and tyrannical. *(Acts for Establishing Religious Freedom in Virginia, 1786.)*

REVOLUTION

The memory of the American Revolution will be immortal, and will immortalize those who record it. *(To D'Auberteuil, 1786.)*

A little rebellion, now and then, is a good thing, and as necessary in the political world as storms in the physical. . . . It is a medicine necessary for the sound health of government. *(To Madison, 1787.)*

The tree of liberty must be refreshed from time to time with the blood of patriots and tyrants. It is its natural manure. *(To Colonel Smith, 1787.)*

What country can preserve its liberties, if its rulers are not warned from time to time that this people preserve the spirit of resistance? Let them take arms. *(Ibid.)*

A great political revolution will take place in your country, and that without bloodshed. *(To Mme. de Brehan, March 14, 1789.)*

Rather than it [the French Revolution] should have failed, I would have seen half the earth desolated; were there but an Adam and an Eve left in every country, and left free, it would be better than as it now is. *(To Wm. Short, 1793.)*

The generation which commences a revolution rarely completes it. *(To Adams, 1823.)*

But when a long train of abuses and usurpations pursuing invariably the same object, evinces a design to reduce them [mankind] under absolute despotism, it is their right, it is their duty, to throw off such Government. *(Declaration of Independence, 1776.)*

TYRANNY

God in heaven will not slumber without end on the iniquities of tyrants. *(To Tench Coxe, 1795.)*

Government, as well as religion, has furnished its schisms, its persecutions, and its devices for fattening idleness on the earnings of the people. . . . In short cannibals are not to be found in the wilds of America only, but are reveling on the blood of every living people. *(To Charles Clay, 1815.)*

Our maxim of that day [1776] was, 'where annual election ends, tyranny begins.' *(To Samuel Adams, 1800.)*

I have sworn upon the altar of God, eternal hostility against every form of tyranny over the mind of man. *(To Dr. Rush, 1800.)*

Seventeen distinct States, amalgamated into one as to their foreign concerns, but single and independent as to their internal administration, regularly organized with a legislature and governor resting on the choice of the people, and enlightened by a free press, can never be so fascinated by the arts of one man, as to submit voluntarily to his usurpation. *(To Destutt de Tracy, 1811.)*

In Europe . . . every man must be either pike or gudgeon, hammer or anvil. *(To C. Hammond, 1821.)*

If ever this vast country is brought under a single government, it will be one of the most extensive corruption. *(To William T. Barry, 1822.)*

What has been the effect of coercion? To make one half the world fools, and the other half hypocrites. *(Notes on Virginia, Query 17.)*

War and Peace

Breaking men to military discipline, is breaking their spirits to principles of passive obedience. *(To J. Hay, 1788.)*

If there be one principle more deeply rooted than any other in the mind of every American, it is that we should have nothing to do with conquest. *(To Wm. Short, 1791.)*

I never expected to be under the necessity of wishing success to Buonaparte. But the English being equally tyrannical at sea as he is on land, and that tyranny bearing on us in every point of either honor or interest, I say, "Down with England." And as for what Buonaparte is then to do to us, let us trust to the chapter of accidents. I cannot, with the Anglomen, prefer a certain present evil to a future hypothetical one. *(To Lieper, 1807.)*

I consider Europe but as a great mad house, and in the present deranged state of their moral faculties to be pitied and avoided. There is no bravery in fighting a maniac. *(To D. B. Warden, 1808: N. Y. Pub. Lib., MS, III, 495-96.)*

Peace is a sublime blessing to men and states. *(To Dr. Griffiths, 1813: ibid., IV, 172.)*

In [Europe] war seems to be the natural state of man. *(To D. B. Warden, 1820.)*

I hope no American patriot will ever lose sight of the essential policy of interdicting in the seas and territories of both Americas, the ferocious and sanguinary contests of Europe. *(To—(?), 1820: N. Y. Pub. Lib., MS, IV, 490.)*

The day is not distant when we may formally require a meridian of partition thro' the ocean which separates the two hemispheres, on the hither side of which no European gust shall ever be heard, nor an American on the other; and when, during the rage of eternal wars of Europe, the lion and the lamb within our regions, shall lie down together in peace. *(Ibid.)*

In the whole animal kingdom I recollect no family but man, steadily and systematically employed in the destruction of itself. . . . The lions and tigers are mere lambs compared with man as a destroyer. *(To Madison, 1797.)*

If they [the European lions and tigers] can so far worry one another as to destroy their power of tyrannizing, the one over the earth, the other the waters, the world may perhaps enjoy peace, till they recruit again. *(To Doctor Benjamin Rush, 1803.)*

What a divine contrast is the calm of our condition to the volcanic state of [Europe]. How do our little party bickerings and squabbles shrink to nothing compared with the fire and sword and havoc of that arena of gladiators. *(To Ticknor, 1816.)*

The hurricane which is now blasting the world, physical and moral, has prostrated all the mounds of reason as well as right. *(To Cæsar Rodney, 1810.)*

When these gladiators [European powers] shall have worried each other into ruin or reason, instead of lying among the dead on the bloody arena, we shall have acquired a growth and strength which will place us *hors d'insulte*. Peace then has been our principle, peace is our interest, and peace has saved to the world this only plant of free and rational government now existing in it. *(To Kosciuszko, 1811.)*

The happiness and prosperity of our citizens . . . , I believe, is the only legitimate object of government, and the first duty of governors, and not the slaughter of men and devastation of the countries placed under their care, in pursuit of a fantastic honor, unallied to virtue or happiness. *(Ibid.)*

A war between Russia and Turkey is like the battle of the kite and snake. Whichever destroys the other, leaves a destroyer the less for the world. *(To Adams, 1822.)*

I hope we shall prove how much happier for man the Quaker policy is, and that the life of the feeder is better than that of the fighter. *(Ibid.)*

Believing that the happiness of mankind is best promoted by the useful pursuits of peace, that on these alone a stable prosperity can be founded, that the evils of war are great in their endurance, and have a long reckoning for ages to come, I have used my best endeavors to keep our country uncommitted in the troubles which afflict Europe, and which assail us on every side. *(To the Republicans of Pittsburgh, 1808.)*

Our lot has been cast, by the favor of heaven, in a country and under circumstances, highly auspicious to our peace and prosperity, and where no pretence can arise for the degrading and oppressive establishments of Europe. *(To the Republican delegates of Washington County, Pennsylvania, 1809.)*

Were the money which it has cost to gain, at the close of a long war, a little town, or a little territory . . . , expended in improving what they already possess, in making roads, opening rivers, building ports, improving the arts, and finding employment for their idle poor, it would render them [the nations] much stronger, much wealthier and happier. This I hope will be our wisdom. *(Notes on Virginia, Query 22.)*

APPENDIX II

OPINION OF CONTEMPORARIES

John Adams

His vanity is a lineament in his character which had entirely escaped me. His want of taste I had observed. Notwithstanding all this he has a sound head on substantial points, and I think he has integrity. . . . At any rate honesty may be extracted even from poisonous weeds. *(To Madison, 1783.)*

He is vain, irritable, and a bad calculator of the force and probable effect of the motives which govern men. This is all the ill which can possibly be said of him. He is as disinterested as the being who made him: he is profound in his views; and accurate in his judgment, except where knowledge of the world is necessary to form a judgment. He is so amiable, that I pronounce you will love him, if ever you become acquainted with him. He would be, as he was, a great man in Congress. *(To Madison, 1787.)*

John Adams was our Colossus on the floor [of Congress]. He was not graceful, nor elegant, nor remarkably fluent, but he came out, occasionally, with a power of thought and expression that moved us from our seats. *(Conversation with Daniel Webster, 1824.)*

SAMUEL ADAMS

For depth of purpose, zeal, and sagacity, no man in Congress exceeded, if any equalled Samuel Adams; and none did more than he to originate and sustain revolutionary measures in Congress. But he could not speak; he had a hesitating, grunting manner. *(Ibid., 1824.)*

I always considered him as more than any other member the fountain of our important measures. And although he was neither an eloquent nor easy speaker, whatever he said was sound and commanded the profound attention of the House. *(To Waterhouse, 1819: N. Y. Pub. Lib., MS, V, 116.)*

ALEXANDER I OF RUSSIA

A more virtuous man, I believe, does not exist, nor one who is more enthusiastically devoted to better the condition of mankind. He will probably, one day, fall a victim to it, as a monarch of that principle does not suit a Russian noblesse. He is not of the very first order of understanding, but he is of a high one. *(To Wm. Duane, 1807.)*

He is young, able, good, and has long years of action still remaining to merit from posterity their devout thanks to heaven that such a ruler has lived. *(To L. Harris, 1817: N. Y. Pub. Lib., MS, IV, 471.)*

I embrace the opportunity of giving expression to the sincere respect and veneration I entertain for your character. It will be among the latest and most soothing comforts of my life, to have seen advanced to the government of so extensive a portion of the earth, and at so early a period of his life, a sovereign whose ruling passion is the advancement of the happiness and prosperity of his people. *(To Czar Alexander I, 1806.)*

EDMUND BURKE

The Revolution of France does not astonish me so much as the revolution of Mr. Burke. I wish I could believe the latter proceeded from as pure motives as the former. . . . How mortifying that this evidence of the rottenness of his mind must oblige us now to ascribe to wicked motives those actions of his life which wore the mark of virtue and patriotism. *(To B. Vaughan, 1791.)*

AARON BURR

His conduct very soon inspired me with distrust. I habitually cautioned Mr. Madison against trusting him too much. *(Anas, 1804.)*

I never thought him an honest, frank-dealing man, but considered him as a crooked gun . . . , whose aim or shot you could never be sure of. *(To Wm. Giles, 1807.)*

A great man in little things, he is really small in great ones. *(To G. Hay, 1807.)*

BENJAMIN FRANKLIN

The ornament of our country and, I may say, of the world. *(To M. Grand, 1790.)*

The greatest man and ornament of the age and country in which he lived. *(To S. Smith, 1798.)*

The father of American philosophy. *(To J. Williams, 1796.)*

Time will be making him greater while it is spunging us from its records. *(To Wm. Smith, 1791.)*

The succession to Dr. Franklin, at the court of France, was an excellent school of humility. On being presented to any one as the minister of America, the commonplace question used in such cases was . . . 'It is you, Sir, who replace Doctor Franklin?' I generally answered, 'No one can replace him, Sir: I am only his successor.' *(To—(?), 1791.)*

FREDERICK WILLIAM II OF PRUSSIA

The bulldog of tyranny. *(To J. Jay, 1789.)*

ALBERT GALLATIN

The ablest man except the President [Madison] who was ever in the administration. *(To Wirt, 1811.)*

There is no truer man than Mr. Gallatin, and after the President, he is the ark of our safety. *(To D. Carr, 1811.)*

Of a pure integrity, and as zealously devoted to the liberties and interests of our country as its most affectionate native citizen. *(To Wm. Duane, 1811.)*

George III

Open your breast, Sire, to liberal and expanded thought. Let not the name of George the Third be a blot on the page of history. *(Rights of British America, 1774.)*

The lunacy of the King of England is a decided fact. *(To Washington, 1788.)*

Our friend George is rather remarkable for doing exactly what he ought not to do. *(To Dr. Ramsay, 1787.)*

The poor maniac George. *(To Mme. de Staël, 1813.)*

George IV

The total of his education was the learning a little Latin, but he speaks French without the slightest accent. . . . He has not a single element of mathematics, of natural or moral philosophy, or any other science on earth, nor has the society he has kept been such as to supply the void of education. It has been of the lowest, the most illiterate and profligate persons of the Kingdom, without choice of rank or mind, and with whom the subjects of conversation are only horses, drinking-matches, bawdy houses, and in terms the most vulgar. . . . He never associated with a man of sense. He has not a single idea of justice, morality, religion, or of the rights of men, or any anxiety for the opinion of the world. . . . He had a fine person, but it is becoming coarse. He possesses good native common sense, is affable, polite and very good humored. *(To J. Jay, 1789.)*

Nathanial Greene

Greene was truly a great man . . . , second to no one in enterprise, in resource, in sound judgment, promptitude of decision, and every other military talent. *(To Wm. Johnson, 1822.)*

Alexander Hamilton

Hamilton is really a colossus to the anti-republican party. Without numbers, he is an host within himself. *(To Madison, 1795.)*

His mind was really powerful, but chained by native partialities to everything English. *(To Wm. Crawford, 1816.)*

Hamilton was indeed a singular character. Of acute understanding, disinterested, honest, and honorable in all private transactions, amiable in society, and duly valuing virtue in private life, yet so bewitched and perverted by the British example, as to be under thorough conviction that corruption was essential to the government of a nation. *(Anas, 1818.)*

Patrick Henry

His manners had something of the coarseness of the society he had frequented; his passion was fiddling, dancing and pleasantry. He excelled in the last, and it attached every one to him. *(To Wm. Wirt, 1815.)*

His eloquence was impressive and sublime. Although it was difficult when he had spoken to tell what he said, yet, while he was speaking, it always seemed directly to the point. . . . He wrote almost nothing—he could not write. . . . He was a man for debate only. *(Conversation with Daniel Webster, 1824.)*

He could not draw a bill on the most simple subject which would bear legal criticism. . . . There was no accuracy of idea in his head. His imagination was copious, poetical, sublime, but vague also. He said the strongest things in the finest language, but without logic, without arrangement, desultorily. *(To Wirt, 1812.)*

Mr. Henry's talents as a popular orator . . . were great indeed; such as I never heard from any other man. He appeared to me to speak as Homer wrote. *(Autobiography, 1821.)*

Andrew Jackson

I feel much alarmed at the prospect of seeing General Jackson President. He is one of the most unfit men I know for such a place. He has had very little respect for laws or constitutions, and is, in fact, an able military chief. His passions are terrible. When I was President of the Senate he was a Senator; and he could never speak on account of the rashness of his feelings. I have seen him attempt it repeatedly, and as often choke with rage. His passions are no doubt cooler now . . . , but he is a dangerous man. *(Conversation with Daniel Webster, 1824.)*

Emperor Joseph II

The Emperor has a head too combustible to be quiet. He is an eccentric character, all enterprise, without principle, without feelings. Ambitious in the extreme but too unsteady to surmount difficulties. *(To Monroe, 1785.)*

Lafayette

He has a great deal of sound genius. . . . His foible is, a canine appetite for popularity and fame, but he will get above this. *(To Madison, 1787.)*

Meriwether Lewis

His talent for observation, which had led him to an accurate knowledge of the plants and animals of his own county, would have distinguished him as a farmer. . . . Of courage undaunted, possessing a firmness and perseverance of purpose which nothing but impossibilities could divert from its direction, careful as a father of those committed to his charge, yet steady in the maintenance of order and discipline, intimate with the Indian character, customs and principles. Habituated to the hunting life, guarded by exact observation of the vegetables and animals of his own country, against losing time in the description of objects already possessed, honest, disinterested, liberal, of sound understanding, and a fidelity to truth so scrupulous that whatever he should report would be as certain as if seen by ourselves. *(To Paul Allen, 1813.)*

Louis XVI

The King is the honestest man in his kingdom, and the most regular and economical.

The King loves business, economy, order and justice, and wishes sincerely the good of his people; but he is irascible, rude, very limited in his understanding, and religious, bordering on bigotry. He has no mistress, loves his queen, and is too much governed by her. *(To Madison, 1787.)*

Louis XVIII

Louis XVIII is a fool and a bigot, but barring a little duplicity he is honest and means well. *(To Monroe, 1816: N. Y. Pub. Lib., MS, IV, 355.)*

James Madison

Trained in these successive schools [Congress and Council], he acquired a habit of self-possession which placed at ready command the rich resources of his luminous and discriminating mind, and of his extensive information, and rendered him the first of every assembly afterwards. . . . Never wandering from his subject into vain declamation, but pursuing it closely in language pure, classical, and copious, soothing always the feelings of his adversaries with civilities and softness of expression, he rose to the eminent station which he held in the great National Convention of 1787 and in that of Virginia which followed. . . . With these consummate powers were united a spotless virtue which no calumny has ever attempted to sully. *(Autobiography, 1821.)*

Marie Antoinette

She is capricious like her brother [Joseph II], and governed by him; devoted to pleasure and expense, and not remarkable for any other vices or virtues. *(To Madison, 1787.)*

This angel, as gaudily painted in the rhapsodies of the Rhetor Burke, with some smartness of fancy, but no sound sense, was proud, disdainful of restraint, indignant at all obstacles to her will, eager in the pursuit of pleasure, and firm enough to hold to her desires, or perish in their wreck. Her inordinate gambling and dissipations . . . had been a sensible item in the exhaustion of the treasury. *(Autobiography, 1821.)*

John Marshall

A crafty chief judge. *(To Ritchie, 1820.)*

His twistifications in the case of Marbury, in that of Burr, and the Yazoo case show how dexterously he can reconcile law to his personal biases. *(To Madison, 1810.)*

Marshall bears [rancorous hatred] to the government of his country. *(Ibid.)*

JAMES MONROE

I clearly think with you on the competence of Monroe to embrace great views of action. *(To Wm. Duane, 1812.)*

He is a man whose soul might be turned wrong side outwards, without discovering a blemish to the world. *(To W. T. Franklin, 1786.)*

I have had, and still have, such entire confidence in the late and present Presidents [Madison and Monroe], that I willingly put both soul and body into their pockets. *(To N. Macon, 1819.)*

NAPOLEON

I considered him as the very worst of all human beings, and as having inflicted more misery on mankind than any other who had ever lived. *(To S. Cathalan, 1816.)*

The Attila of the age dethroned, the ruthless destroyer of ten millions of the human race, whose thirst for blood appeared unquenchable, the great oppressor of the rights and liberties of the world, shut up within the circle of a little island. . . . How miserably, how meanly, has he closed his inflated career! . . . He should have perished on the swords of his enemies, under the walls of Paris. But Buonaparte was a lion in the field only. In civil life a cold-blooded, calculating, unprincipled usurper, without a virtue; no statesman, knowing nothing of commerce, political economy, or civil government, and supplying ignorance by bold presumption. *(To Adams, 1814.)*

I believe the loss of the battle of Waterloo was the salvation of France. Had Buonaparte obtained the victory, his talents, his egoism, and destitution of all moral principle, would have rivetted a military despotism on your necks. *(To Lafayette, 1816: N. Y. Pub. Lib., MS, IV, 369.)*

He wanted totally the sense of right and wrong. If he could consider the millions of human lives which he had destroyed or caused to be destroyed, the desolations of countries by plunderings, burnings, and famine, the destitutions of lawful rulers of the world without the consent of their constituents . . . , the cutting up of established societies of men and jumbling them discordantly together again at his caprice, the demolition of the fairest hopes of mankind for the recovery of their rights and amelioration of their condition, and all the numberless train of his other enormities; the man, I say, who could consider all these as no crime, must have been a moral monster, against whom every hand should have been lifted to slay him. *(To Adams, 1823.)*

The penance he is now doing for all his atrocities must be soothing to every virtuous heart. It proved that we have a god in heaven. That he is just, and not careless of what passes in this world. And we cannot but wish to this inhuman wretch, a long, long life, that time as well as intensity may fill up his sufferings to the measure of his atrocities. But indeed what sufferings can atone for his crimes against the liberties and happiness of the human race; for the miseries he has already inflicted on his own generation, and on those yet to come, on whom he has rivetted the chains of despotism! *(To Ticknor, 1817.)*

Jacques Necker

Eloquence in a high degree, knowledge in matters of account and order, are distinguishing traits in his character. Ambition is his first passion, virtue his second. He has not discovered that sublime truth, that a bold, unequivocal virtue is the best handmaid even to ambition. . . . His judgment is not of the first order, scarcely even of the second; his resolution frail; and, upon the whole, it is rare to meet an instance of a person so much below the reputation he has obtained. . . .

Nature bestowed on Necker an ardent passion for glory, without, at the same time, granting him those qualities required for its pursuit by direct means. The union of a fruitful imagination with a limited talent. . . . His riches, his profession, his table, and a virtuous, reasonable and well-informed wife, procured him the acquaintance of many persons of distinction. . . . Not at all delicate in the choice of his means, he succeeded to his wish in his object, which was the establishing himself in public opinion. . . .

All these circumstances reared for him an astonishing reputation. . . . People will not reflect, that, in the short period

of his ministry, he had more than doubled his fortune. . . .
I would compare him to a steward, who, by his management,
does not entirely ruin his master, but who enriches himself at
his expense. *(To John Jay, 1789.)*

Madame Necker

Mme. Necker was a very sincere and excellent woman, but
she was not very pleasant in conversation, for she was subject
to what in Virginia we call the 'Budge,' that is, she was very
nervous and fidgety. She could rarely remain long in the same
place, or converse long on the same subject. I have known
her to get up from table five or six times in the course of the
dinner, and walk up and down her saloon to compose herself.
(Conversation with Daniel Webster, 1824.)

Thomas Paine

They [Lord Bolingbroke and Paine] were alike in making
bitter enemies of the priests and pharisees of their day.
Both were honest men; both advocates for human liberty.
. . . No writer has exceeded Paine in ease and familiarity of
style, in perspicacity of expression, happiness of elucidation,
and in simple and unassuming language. In this he may be
compared with Dr. Franklin. *(To F. Eppes, 1821.)*

Paine thought more than he read. *(To J. Cartwright, 1824.)*

Maximilien Robespierre

What a tremendous obstacle to the future attempts at
liberty will be the atrocities of Robespierre! *(To T. Coxe, 1795.)*

Robespierre met the fate, and his memory the execration,
he so justly merited. *(To Mme. de Staël, 1813.)*

Comte de Vergennes

He is a great minister in European affairs, but has very imperfect ideas of our institutions, and no confidence in them.
His devotion to the principles of pure despotism, renders him
unaffectionate to our government. But his fear of England
makes him value us as a make weight. He is cool, reserved in
political conversations, but free and familiar on other subjects,
and a very attentive, agreeable person to do business with.

It is impossible to have a clearer, better organized head; but age has chilled his heart. *(To Madison, 1787.)*

George Washington

His mind was great and powerful, without being of the very first order; his penetration strong, though not so acute as that of a Newton, Bacon, or Locke; and as far as he saw, no judgment was ever sounder. It was slow in operation, being little aided by invention or imagination, but sure in conclusion. . . . Hearing all suggestions, he selected whatever was best; and certainly no General ever planned his battles more judiciously. But if deranged during the course of the action . . . he was slow in readjustment. . . . He was incapable of fear, meeting personal dangers with the calmest unconcern.

Perhaps the strongest feature in his character was prudence, never acting until every circumstance, every consideration was maturely weighed. . . . His integrity was most pure, his justice the most inflexible I have ever known, no motives of interest or consanguinity, of friendship or hatred, being able to bias his decision. He was, indeed, in every sense of the words, a wise, a good, and a great man. His temper was naturally irritable and high toned; but reflection and resolution had obtained a firm and habitual ascendancy over it. If ever, however, it broke its bonds, he was most tremendous in his wrath.

In his expenses he was honorable, but exact; liberal in contributions to whatever promised utility; but frowning and unyielding on all visionary projects and all unworthy calls on his charity. His heart was not warm in its affections; but he exactly calculated every man's value, and gave him a solid esteem proportioned to it.

His person, you know, was fine, his stature exactly what one would wish, his deportment easy, erect and noble; the best horseman of his age, and the most graceful figure that could be seen on horseback.

Although in the circle of his friends, where he might be unreserved with safety, he took a free share in conversation, his colloquial talents were not above mediocrity, possessing neither copiousness of ideas, nor fluency of words. In public, when called on for a sudden opinion, he was unready, short and embarrassed. Yet he wrote readily, rather diffusely, in an easy and correct style. This he had acquired by conversation with the world, for his education was merely reading, writing and common arithmetic, to which he added surveying at a later day. His time was employed in action chiefly, reading little, and that only in agriculture and English history. . . . His agricultural proceedings occupied most of his leisure hours within doors.

On the whole, his character was, in its mass, perfect, in nothing bad, in few points indifferent; and it may truly be said, that never did nature and fortune combine more perfectly to make a man great, and to place him . . . in an everlasting remembrance. *(To Dr. W. Jones, 1814.)*

Daniel Webster

I am much gratified by the acquaintance of Mr. Webster. He is likely to become a great weight in our government. *(To Monroe, 1824.)*

Noah Webster

I view Webster as a mere pedagogue, of very limited understanding and very strong prejudices and party passions. *(To Madison, 1801.)*

George Wythe

No man ever left behind him a character more venerated than George Wythe. His virtue was of the purest tint; his integrity inflexible and his justice exact; of warm patriotism, and, devoted as he was to liberty and the natural and equal rights of man, he might truly be called the Cato of his country, without the avarice of the Roman, for a more disinterested person never lived. *(J. Saunderson, 1820.)*

INDEX

Adams, John, 172
Adams, Samuel, 173
Africa, 101, 102, 103
Agriculture (and farmers), 33, 54, 68-71, 84, 85, 87, 89, 104, 105, 106, 126, 140, 150, 159
Alexander I of Russia, 173
America, 25, 27, 29, 30-31, 36, 41, 43, 56, 57, 62, 66, 70, 74, 76, 81-83, 86, 90, 92, 93, 101, 102, 103, 115, 130, 131, 133, 138, 142, 146-7, 151, 163, 164, 166, 169
Antoninus, emperor, 23
Aristocrats and Aristocracy, 22, 42, 43, 44, 45, 79, 80, 86, 91, 135, 136, 138, 142, 150
Aristotle, 21, 22, 117
Arminians, 109
Army, 31, 47, 48, 49, 67, 75, 86, 132, 153
Athanasius, 167
Austria, 26, 131

Bacon, Francis, 182
Banking, 76-9
Baptists, 115, 119
Berlin, 25
Bill of Rights, 14, 47-52, 57
Blackstone, Sir William, 84, 85
Bolingbroke, Viscount, 181
Bonaparte, Napoleon, 21, 85, 97, 98, 124, 125, 130, 134, 135, 136, 142, 143, 146, 164, 170, 179-80.
Boston, 134
Bourbons, 26
Brazil, 147
Brissotins, 137
Brutus, 22
Buffon, Georges Louis Leclerc, Comte de, 16
Burke, Edmund, 173-4, 178
Burr, Aaron, 174, 178

Cabinet, 60
Caesar, Julius, 22
Caligula, 124
Calvinism, 109, 119, 120, 122, 166, 167
Catharine II of Russia, 26
Catiline, Lucius Sergius, 124
Cato, Marcus Portius, 22, 183
Charles IV of Spain, 26
China, 69
Christian VII of Denmark, 26
Christianity. See Religion
Cicero, Marus Tullius, 22
Cincinnati Society, 80, 81
Classes (social), 79-86
Clergy. See Religion
Coke, Sir Edward, 84
Commerce (and manufacture), 30, 31, 32, 33, 54, 68, 69, 74, 76, 126, 127, 128, 134, 136, 151, 153, 159
Congress. See Legislature
Connecticut, 43, 63, 84
Constantinople, 109
Constitution (American), 14, 23, 30, 31, 34, 35, 38, 43, 46-68, 76, 77, 79, 80, 84, 86, 96, 108, 116, 152-3, 166

Copenhagen, 134
Cuba, 147

Danton, Georges Jacques, 28, **137**
Debt, public, 15, 16, 31, 33, **71, 74,** 77, 78, 159
Declaration of Independence, **13,** 13-2n, 14, 83
Democratic party. See Republican party
Denmark, 26, 131
Descartes, René, 110
Despotism, 14, 23, 30, 32, 34, 46, 55, 56, 64, 84, 88, 98, 126, 133, 136, 141, 143, 144, 145, 146, 147, 154, 161, 169, 179-80, 181
Dictatorship, 52, 53, 65, 66
Directory, French, 59

Economy, 31, 33
Education, 23, 33, 83, 87-92, 99, 118, 146, 149
England, 15, 19, 22, 23, 25, 26, 43, 44, 46, 48, 56, 66, 73, 77, 78, 79, 81, 84, 85, 86, 87, 91, 92, 118, 119, 121, 125, 127, 131, 133-8, 147, 148, 149-50, 151, 155, 170, 176, 181
Entangling alliances, 31, 32, 126-133, 151
Equality, 13, 29, 35, 79, 81, 82, 83, 150-1
Euclid, 119
Europe, 21, 24, 25, 26, 27, 31, 39, 44, 45, 56, 57, 64, 67, 69, 70, 71, 77, 81, 82, 84, 85, 86, 90-2, 93, 97, 101, 103, 104, 114, 115, 123-48, 149, 151, 156, 170-1
Executive. See Presidency

Farmers. See Agriculture
Federal government, 30-1, 43, 50, 51, 52, 53-5, 64, 65, 95, 122
Federalist, The, 153
Federalists, 43, 44, 45, 58, 164
Ferdinand IV of Naples, 26
Finance, 73, 76, 77, 102, 158-160
Fontainebleau, 139
France (see also Revolution, French), 21, 23, 25, 28, 40, 53, 56, 58n, 59, 78, 81, 107, 110, 117, 121, 125, 130, 131, 138-44, 146, 151, 174, 179
Franklin, Benjamin, 174, 181
Frederick the Great, 26
Frederick William II of Prussia, 26, 174
Freedom (of person), 13, 14, 33, 34, 37, 38, 45, 47, 51, 83, 99, 101, 108, 113, 130, 154
Freedom of the press. See Press

Galileo, 110
Gallatin, Albert, 174, **175**
Genoa, 39
George III of England, 26, 135, 175
George IV of England, 175
Germans, 100
Germany, 56, 131
Girondists, 137

184

INDEX

Greece, 21, 86
Greene, Nathanial, 175
Gustavus III of Sweden, 26

Habeas corpus, 33, 37, 47, 48, 67
Hamilton, Alexander, 159, 176
Henry, Patrick, 176
Holland, 40, 131, 146
Homer, 99-100, 176
House of Representatives. *See* Legislature
Howe, Viscount William, 134
Hume, David, 33, 85

Immigration, 107-8
Impeachment, 48, 63, 64, 65
Indians (American), 15, 19, 25, 39, 93, 103-7, 177
Industry, 54, 68, 89, 129, 158, 159
Italy, 22, 131
Iturbide, Augustin de, 21

Jackson, Andrew, 176-7
Jacobins, 42, 43, 137
Jefferson, Thomas, member of Washington's cabinet, 60, 61; as President, 60; and Virginia reform bills, 83; conversation with a French working woman, 139-40; and Franklin, 174
Jesus, 116, 117, 118, 119, 120-1, 122, 166, 167, 168
Jews (and Jewish religion), 116, 117, 120, 121, 122
Joseph II of Austria, 26, 177, 178
Judiciary, 40, 41, 46, 49, 52, 61-6, 152
Jury, trial by, 14, 33, 37, 47, 48, 62, 67, 137, 160
Justice, 18, 29, 32, 38, 39, 40, 61, 109, 125, 158

Kings. *See* Monarchy

Labor, 33, 44, 68, 69-70, 74, 75, 76, 78, 79, 80, 81, 85, 86, 88, 99, 150, 160
Lafayette, Marquis de, 177
Law, 16, 17, 18, 34, 39, 61, 67, 81, 91, 93, 107, 109, 152-3
Lawyers, 16, 84, 85, 150
Legislature, 15, 17, 18, 35, 40, 46, 47, 48, 50, 51, 52, 55, 61, 62, 63, 66, 75, 83, 115, 152, 153
Lewis, Meriwether, 177
Liberty, 13, 19, 20, 21, 33, 57, 62, 73, 80, 84, 85, 89, 96, 98, 99, 126, 129, 132, 137, 141, 143, 144, 151, 153-6, 168, 181, 183
Lincoln, Abraham, 147
Livy, Titus, 124
Locke, John, 182
London, 25
Louis XVI of France, 26, 27, 137, 140, 141, 177, 178
Louis XVIII of France, 21, 178
Loyola, Ignatius, 167

Machiavelli, Niccolo, 124
Madison, James, 67, 95n, 174, 178, 179

Madrid, 25
Majority rule, 15, 16, 18, 23, 32, 33, 34, 40, 53, 61, 161, 163
Marat, Jean Paul, 137
Marie Antoinette, 178
Marshall, John, 178, 179
Maryland, 102
Massachusetts, 23, 43, 84, 165
Merchants, 84, 158
Methodists, 119
Mexico, 148
Militarism, 32, 34
Militia, 31, 32, 48, 53, 67, 153
Minority rights, 33, 34
Monarchy, 19, 21, 24-7, 44, 45, 50, 56, 57, 66, 81, 84, 87, 91, 107, 130, 132, 142, 156
Monocrats, 43
Monopolies, 47, 49
Monroe, James, 179
Montaigne, Michel Eyquem de, 38
Montesquieu, Charles De Secondat, Baron de, 23, 29, 36
Morality (moral sense, moral instinct, moral principle), 17, 31, 37, 39, 66, 99, 101, 116, 119, 124, 125, 129, 134, 138, 158, 164-5, 180

Naples, 26
Napoleon. *See* Bonaparte
Natural rights, 13-9, 45, 67, 68, 71, 72, 74, 80, 86, 95, 107, 113, 114, 160, 165, 183
Navy, 31, 75, 153
Necker, Jacques, 180-1
Necker, Mme., 181
Negroes. *See* Slavery
Nero, 95
Neutrality, 127-9, 133
New England, 39, 43, 115, 122
New York, 58n, 111
Newton, Sir Isaac, 101, 104, 110, 182

Paine, Thomas, 181
Papacy, 56
Paris, 137, 141, 179
Patriotism, 157, 168, 174
Peace, 31, 32, 33, 74, 77, 105, 106, 125, 129, 132, 138, 145, 147, 151, 170-2
Pendleton, Edmund, 49
Pennsylvania, 43, 111
Platonism, 117, 118, 122
Poland, 39, 47, 56
Political parties, 42-5
Portugal, 26, 131
Presbyterians, 119, 120
Presidency, 40, 43, 46, 47n, 50, 51, 55-61, 62, 63, 65, 66, 116, 132, 152
Press, 31, 33, 34, 37, 47, 52, 67, 89, 92-98, 132, 163-4, 169
Priests (*see also* Religion), 16, 21, 40, 44, 45, 84, 87, 112, 117, 122, 142, 144, 146, 165, 167, 181
Property, right of, 15-6, 18, 34, 48, 99, 100, 101, 106, 139-140
Prussia, 26, 131

INDEX

Public opinion, 13n, 31, 33, 37, 39, 63, 89, 90, 93, 94, 95-6, 115, 120, 164, 165, 180
Public works, 54, 55

Quakers, 76, 100, 117, 118, 119, 124, 171

Religion, 29, 31, 33, 84, 93, 94, 108-23, 165-8, 169
Religion, freedom of, 31, 33, 34, 37, 47, 67, 109-16
Republic (and republicanism), 18, 22, 24-5, 28, 29, 32, 36, 39-42, 50, 57, 64, 65, 76, 90, 129, 142, 144, 152, 156, 162
Republican (Democratic) party, 45
Revolution, 14, 19, 20, 21, 22, 23, 32, 33, 37, 47, 66, 68, 73, 146, 159, 164, 168-9
Revolution, American, 33, 52, 80, 141, 168
Revolution, French, 20, 28, 32, 34, 141-2, 143, 168, 169
Robespierre, Maximilien, 21, 28
Rochefoucauld, François, Duc de la, 38
Roman Empire, 22-3, 56, 86, 90, 95, 103, 110
Russia, 123, 124, 131, 146, 171, 173

Sallust, 124
Santo Domingo, 102
Sardinia, 26
Science, 31, 32, 82, 88-9, 90, 96, 104, 126, 131, 143
Self-government, 13, 15, 18, 19, 21, 22, 24, 27, 33, 36, 65, 96, 129, 144, 145, 146, 147, 160-3
Servetus, Michael, 119
Slavery (Negro), 14, 85, 86, 98-103, 146, 158
Socrates, 121
South America. *See* Spanish America
Spain, 26, 131, 146
Spanish America, 21, 133, 144-148
State governments, 30, 32, 33, 36, 40, 50, 51, 52-5, 64, 65, 67, 152, 163, 169

States' rights, 31, 52-5
Suffrage, 38
Supreme Court (*see also* Judiciary), 63-4, 65, 152
Sweden, 26, 131
Switzerland, 39, 131

Tacitus, Caius Cornelius, 124
Tarquin, Lucius, 124
Taxation, 37, 46, 47, 73, 74-6, 78, 79, 159
Titus, Flavius Vespasianus, 23
Toleration, 34, 35, 44, 108-17, 154, 167
Tories, 42, 43, 85
Trajan, Marcus Ulpius, 23
Turgot, Anne Robert Jacques, 124
Turkey, 23, 56, 123, 124, 171
Tyranny, 18-19, 22, 28, 55, 74, 88, 98, 108, 111, 112, 115, 131, 162, 168, 169-70

Union. *See* Federal government
United States. *See* America

Venice, 39, 40
Vergennes, Charles Gravier, Comte de, 181-2
Versailles, 25
Victor Amadeus III of Sardinia, 26
Vienna, 25
Violence, 44, 101, 125
Virginia, 15, 43, 49, 57, 100, 101, 112, 120, 178, 181
Voltaire, 138

War, 31, 32, 48, 69, 73, 74, 75, 77, 78, 105, 123-33, 134, 138, 145, 147, 148, 151, 159, 161, 170-2
Washington, city of, 64, 163
Washington, George, 57-9, 60, 80, 182-3
Waterloo, 179
Webster, Daniel, 183
Webster, Noah, 183
Whigs, 42, 43
William and Mary College, 91
Wythe, George, 49, 91, 183